From Side Hustle to Full-Time Gig

Freelancing 101

ZACH C. ANDY

ZACH C. ANDY EXPERIENCE

CONTENTS

CHAPTER 1

The Power of Freelancing

In a world where traditional employment structures are shifting, freelancing has emerged as a powerful alternative career path. The allure of flexibility, independence, and the pursuit of a better work-life balance has drawn many individuals to embrace the freelance lifestyle. This chapter explores the personal experiences and motivations that lead people to pursue freelancing as a full-time career, as well as the benefits and opportunities that freelancing offers compared to traditional employment.

The decision to transition from a structured professional environment to freelancing is often driven by a desire for flexibility and independence. The freedom to choose when and where to work allows individuals to better manage personal commitments and pursue projects that align with their passions. Being their own boss and taking ownership of their work is highly appealing, as freelancing provides the opportunity to have full control over decision-making, work directly with clients, and have a direct impact on the success of their own business.

The entrepreneurial spirit also plays a significant role in the decision to pursue freelancing. The challenge of building one's own business, exploring new opportunities, and continuously learning and growing professionally is an exciting prospect. Moreover, freelancing offers the chance to create a better work-life balance, prioritizing personal commitments, spending quality time with loved ones, and pursuing hobbies and interests while still earning a living doing what one loves.

Freelancing offers several benefits and opportunities compared to traditional employment. One of the biggest advantages is flexibility. Freelancers have control over their schedule, allowing them to choose when, where, and how much they work. This flexibility enables a better work-life balance and the ability to accommodate personal commitments. Additionally, freelancers have the independence to make decisions, set their own rates, and choose the projects they work on. This autonomy allows for greater control over professional growth and the direction of one's career.

The variety and diverse experiences that freelancing offers are also significant benefits. Freelancers have the opportunity to work on a variety of projects with different clients, continually learning and expanding their skill set across various industries. This diversity provides exposure to different challenges and perspectives, fostering personal and professional growth. Furthermore, freelancers have the potential to earn more compared to traditional employment. They can set their own rates based on their skills, experience, and the value they provide. With the ability to take on multiple clients and projects, freelancers can increase their income and achieve financial independence.

Freelancing also provides individuals with professional autonomy. They can choose the type of work they want to do, select clients that align with their values, and define their own career path. This autonomy fosters a sense of fulfillment and satisfaction in one's work. Additionally, freelancing often offers the option to work remotely, providing the freedom to work from anywhere in the world. This eliminates the need for a daily commute and allows freelancers to design their ideal work environment.

Continuous learning and skill development are inherent in freelancing. Freelancers are constantly exposed to new challenges and projects, requiring ongoing learning and skill development. This enables them to stay ahead of industry trends, expand their knowledge base, and remain competitive in their field. Freelancing also allows individuals to build a diverse network of clients, collaborators, and industry professionals. Networking can lead to new business opportunities, referrals, and collaborations that can further enhance a freelancer's career prospects.

While freelancing offers numerous benefits, there are also challenges and misconceptions that individuals commonly face. Irregular income is one of the main challenges freelancers encounter. To overcome this, freelancers can create a budget, establish an emergency fund, and diversify their client base. Finding clients can also be a hurdle, but freelancers can develop a strong online presence, leverage freelance platforms and job boards, and seek referrals from existing clients. Self-motivation and time management are crucial skills for freelancers, and they can be fostered through setting clear goals, utilizing productivity tools, and establishing boundaries between work and personal life.

Building a strong brand and reputation is essential for freelancers to stand out in a competitive market. This can be achieved by defining a clear niche, investing in personal branding, and consistently delivering high-quality work. The feeling of loneliness and lack of support is another challenge that freelancers face, but they can overcome it by joining freelancer communities, attending industry events, and engaging in collaborative projects or partnerships. Managing administrative tasks is also a challenge, but freelancers can use technology tools, automate repetitive tasks, and consider outsourcing certain administrative tasks.

Freelancing empowers individuals to take control of their careers and achieve their goals. It provides flexibility, autonomy, and opportunities for professional growth and skill development. Freelancers have the potential to earn more, expand their network, and integrate work into their desired lifestyle. By addressing the challenges and misconceptions associated with freelancing, individuals can overcome obstacles and build a successful freelance career. Freelancing is a powerful path that allows individuals to leverage their skills and experiences while embracing new opportunities in the ever-evolving world of freelancing.

CHAPTER 2

Assessing Skills and Finding Your Niche

In the vast world of freelancing, it is essential to assess your skills and find your niche to position yourself effectively and thrive in the market. This chapter will explore the importance of self-assessment, researching market demand, and identifying a target audience. It will also delve into the factors to consider when choosing a niche and positioning yourself as an expert. Finally, it will provide examples of freelancers who have successfully identified their niche and built thriving businesses around it, as well as strategies for staying adaptable and evolving as market demands change.

Self-Assessment: Unearthing Your Core Skills and Interests

Before embarking on your freelancing journey, it is crucial to engage in self-assessment exercises that help you gain clarity about your strengths, passions, and areas of expertise. By understanding your skills and interests, you can align them with market demand and find a niche that suits you best. Here are some recommended self-assessment exercises:

Skills Inventory:

Begin by making a comprehensive list of all the skills you possess, both technical and soft skills. Evaluate your proficiency level for each skill and identify the ones you enjoy using the most. Consider your past work experiences, hobbies, and educational background to identify transferable skills.

Values and Interests Assessment:

Reflect on your personal values and what is important to you in your work. Consider your hobbies, activities, and subjects you enjoy learning about. Identify the industries or fields that align with your interests and values.

SWOT Analysis:

Conduct a SWOT (Strengths, Weaknesses, Opportunities, Threats) analysis for yourself. Identify your strengths and weaknesses in terms of skills, experience, and personal qualities. Evaluate the opportunities and potential threats in the freelance market or specific industries of interest.

Feedback and Reflection:

Seek feedback from colleagues, mentors, or clients on your strengths and areas of expertise. Reflect on past projects or experiences that brought you satisfaction and success. Consider the tasks or projects that energize you and make you feel fulfilled.

Market Research:

Explore the current demand for different freelance skills in the market. Research industry trends, emerging technologies, and areas with growth potential. Identify the skills that are in high demand and align with your interests.

Online Assessments and Tools:

Use online tools or assessments that can help identify your strengths, personality traits, or preferred working styles. Assessments like Myers-Briggs Type Indicator (MBTI), StrengthsFinder, or DISC can provide insights into your personality and preferences.

Journaling and Self-Reflection:

Dedicate time for journaling or self-reflection exercises to explore your passions, interests, and skills. Write down your thoughts, experiences, and achievements to gain insights into what energizes and motivates you.

By engaging in these self-assessment exercises, you can gain a clearer understanding of your core skills and interests. This self-awareness will help you identify your target audience, niche, and position yourself effectively in the freelancing market.

Researching Market Demand and Identifying a Target Audience

Once you have assessed your skills and interests, it is essential to research market demand and identify a target audience for your freelancing services. This research will help you understand the demand for specific services and tailor your offerings to meet the needs of your target audience. Here are the recommended steps:

Determine Your Skills and Interests:

Start by assessing your own skills, expertise, and interests. This self-reflection will help you understand what services you can offer and which industries or niches align with your strengths.

Conduct Market Research:

Researching the market is crucial to identify the demand for specific freelance services. Use various resources such as industry reports, online forums, social media groups, and freelance job platforms to gather insights on the demand for different services. Analyze trends, competition, and pricing in your target industry.

Define Your Target Audience:

Once you have identified the demand for your services, narrow down your target audience. Consider factors such as demographics, industries, company sizes, and specific pain points to define your ideal clients. Understanding the needs and preferences of your target audience will help you tailor your services and marketing efforts effectively.

Seek Feedback and Validation:

It is important to seek feedback from potential clients or industry professionals. Share your service offerings with your target audience or network and ask for input. This feedback can help you refine your offerings and ensure they align with market demand.

Utilize Online Platforms and Communities:

Online platforms like LinkedIn, industry-specific forums, and social media groups provide opportunities to connect with professionals in your target industry. By participating in discussions, sharing valuable insights, and offering assistance, you can establish yourself as an expert in your field and build relationships with potential clients.

Conduct Pilot Projects:

Consider offering your services on a trial basis or at discounted rates to a select group of clients. This approach allows you to gain practical experience, receive testimonials, and further validate your offerings in the market.

By following these steps, you can conduct thorough market research, identify a target audience, and position yourself effectively to meet the demand for your services.

Choosing a Niche and Positioning Yourself as an Expert

Choosing a niche and positioning yourself as an expert is crucial for freelancers to stand out in a crowded market. By specializing in a specific area, you can attract clients who value your expertise and are willing to pay a premium for your services.

Here are the factors to consider when choosing a niche and positioning yourself as an expert:

Passion and Expertise:

Choose a niche that aligns with your passion and expertise. By focusing on something you are genuinely interested in and have deep knowledge about, you can provide high-quality services and stand out as an expert in your field.

Market Demand:

Assess the demand for your chosen niche. Research the market to understand if there is a viable client base and sufficient demand for your services. It is beneficial to choose a niche where there is a balance between demand and competition.

Target Audience:

Understand the needs, pain points, and preferences of your target audience. Consider who your ideal clients are and how your niche aligns with their specific requirements. Positioning yourself as the go-to expert for a particular audience can help attract clients more effectively.

Unique Value Proposition:

Identify your unique value proposition within your chosen niche. Determine what sets you apart from competitors and why clients should choose you over others. This could be a specific skill set, industry experience, innovative approaches, or a unique perspective.

Market Trends and Future Prospects:

Consider the current market trends and future growth potential within your chosen niche. Ensure that your niche is not only relevant now but also has long-term sustainability and opportunities for growth.

Competition Analysis:

Evaluate the competition within your chosen niche. Assess the existing players, their strengths, weaknesses, pricing strategies, and marketing approaches. This analysis will help you differentiate yourself and find a unique positioning angle.

Branding and Marketing Strategy:

Develop a strong personal brand that reflects your expertise and resonates with your target audience. This includes creating a compelling brand story, designing a professional website or portfolio, utilizing social media platforms effectively, and developing thought leadership content to establish credibility.

By considering these factors, you can choose a niche that aligns with your passion and expertise, position yourself as an expert, and attract clients who value your specialized skills and knowledge.

Examples of Successful Niche Identification and Business Building

To provide inspiration, here are a few examples of freelancers who have successfully identified their niche and built thriving businesses around it:

1. Graphic Design for Sustainable Brands:

A freelancer with a passion for sustainability and design may identify the niche of providing graphic design services specifically tailored to sustainable brands. By positioning themselves as an expert in this niche, they can attract clients who value environmentally friendly design and build a reputation within the sustainability industry.

2. Social Media Management for Health and Wellness Professionals:

A freelancer with experience and knowledge in the health and wellness industry may choose to specialize in social media management for health coaches, yoga instructors, and nutritionists. By understanding the unique needs and target audience of this industry, they can provide tailored social media strategies and content creation specifically for health and wellness professionals.

3. Copywriting for Tech Startups:

A freelancer with a background in technology and a knack for writing may identify the niche of providing copywriting services to tech startups. They can position themselves as an expert in crafting compelling and technical content that appeals to startup founders, investors, and technology enthusiasts.

4. Virtual Assistance for Real Estate Agents:

A freelancer with administrative skills may choose to specialize in providing virtual assistance services specifically for real estate agents. By understanding the needs and demands of real estate professionals, they can offer services such as managing listings, coordinating appointments, and handling administrative tasks unique to the industry.

5. Video Editing for Travel Vloggers:

A freelancer with expertise in video editing and a passion for travel may carve out a niche by offering video editing services tailored to travel vloggers. They can showcase their skills in creating captivating travel videos, understanding the storytelling aspect of vlogs, and providing editing services that enhance the travel experience.

In each of these examples, freelancers have identified a niche that combines their skills, interests, and market demand. By positioning themselves as experts within these niches, they attract clients who recognize the value of their specialized services and build a thriving business by catering to their specific needs.

Staying Adaptable and Evolving as Market Demands Change

In the ever-evolving freelance landscape, it is crucial to stay adaptable and evolve as market demands change. Here are some strategies to help you stay ahead of the curve:

Continuous Learning:

Always be open to learning and upgrading your skills. Stay up to date with industry trends, attend webinars or workshops, take online courses, and seek professional certifications. By staying ahead of the curve, you can adapt to changing market demands and offer new services or approaches as needed.

Regular Self-Assessment:

Regularly assess your skills, strengths, and weaknesses. Identify areas where you may need improvement or expansion. Recognize your limitations and seek opportunities to upskill or collaborate with other freelancers who complement your skill set.

Networking and Collaboration:

Build a strong professional network. Connect with other freelancers, industry professionals, and potential clients. Gain insights into emerging market trends and collaborate on projects that require a diverse skill set. Collaborative partnerships can help you expand your service offerings and tap into new markets.

Diversification of Services:

Instead of relying solely on one niche or service, diversify your offerings. Cater to a wider range of clients and adapt to changing market demands. For example, a freelance graphic designer may start offering website design services or branding consultations to expand their service portfolio.

Market Research and Analysis:

Conduct regular market research. Stay informed about evolving client needs and industry trends. Analyze market demands, competitors, and emerging technologies or techniques. Proactively identify opportunities for growth and adjust your strategies accordingly.

Client Feedback and Communication:

Actively seek feedback from clients. Understand their evolving needs and expectations. Maintain regular communication to stay updated on changing project requirements, industry challenges, and emerging trends. Adapt your services to meet evolving demands effectively.

Embrace Technology and Tools:

Leverage technology and productivity tools that streamline your work processes and enhance efficiency. Embrace project management software, collaboration tools, automation tools, and industry-specific software or platforms. Adapt to changing market dynamics and deliver high-quality work more effectively.

By implementing these strategies, you can stay adaptable in the face of changing market demands. Continuously evolve your skills, diversify your services, collaborate with others, and leverage technology to ensure long-term success in the dynamic freelance landscape.

Assessing your skills, finding your niche, and positioning yourself as an expert are crucial steps in building a successful freelancing career. Through self-assessment exercises and market research, you can align your skills and interests with market demand and identify a target audience. By choosing a niche that combines your passion and expertise, you can stand out in a crowded market and attract clients who value your specialized services. Staying adaptable and evolving as market demands change is essential for long-term success. By continuously learning, networking, diversifying your services, and embracing technology, you can thrive in the ever-evolving freelance landscape.

CHAPTER 3

Setting Goals and Creating a Business Plan

Setting goals is an essential step for freelancers to achieve success in their ventures. Without clear goals, freelancers may lack direction and struggle to measure their progress. In this chapter, we will explore practical tips for setting achievable goals and creating a comprehensive business plan that will serve as a roadmap for success.

Setting Achievable Goals

To set achievable goals, freelancers should follow these practical tips:

1. Be Specific:

It is crucial to clearly define goals to ensure clarity and focus. Instead of setting a general goal like "increase client base," set a specific goal such as "acquire five new clients within the next three months." Specific goals provide a clear direction and make it easier to measure progress.

2. Make Them Measurable:

Goals should be measurable objectively. Instead of setting a goal like "improve client satisfaction," set a measurable goal like "achieve a client satisfaction rating of 90% or higher based on client feedback surveys." Measurable goals allow freelancers to track their progress and determine whether they have achieved them.

3. Set Realistic and Attainable Goals:

It is important to set goals that are realistic and attainable based on current capabilities, resources, and market conditions. Setting unrealistic or overly ambitious goals can lead to frustration and demotivation. Consider factors such as workload, available time, and market demand when determining what is achievable.

4. Break Them Down into Smaller Milestones:

Breaking down larger goals into smaller, actionable milestones helps create a roadmap and makes goals more manageable. Each milestone achieved provides a sense of accomplishment and motivation to keep moving forward.

5. Set Deadlines:

Assigning deadlines to goals and milestones creates a sense of urgency and helps freelancers stay focused and accountable. Deadlines should be reasonable and allow for sufficient time to complete necessary tasks.

6. Write Them Down:

Documenting goals in writing increases commitment and helps freelancers stay organized. Keeping goals visible, such as on a vision board or in a journal, serves as a constant reminder of what they are working towards.

7. Regularly Review and Adjust:

Periodically reviewing goals allows freelancers to assess progress and make necessary adjustments. Market conditions or personal circumstances may change, requiring modifications to goals. Regular review allows for flexibility and adaptation to new opportunities or challenges.

8. Celebrate Achievements:

Recognizing and celebrating each milestone or goal achieved boosts motivation and reinforces a positive mindset. Celebrating successes also instills a belief in the ability to achieve future goals.

By following these practical tips, freelancers can set achievable goals that provide direction, motivation, and a roadmap for success in their freelance ventures.

Creating a Comprehensive Business Plan

In addition to setting goals, freelancers should create a comprehensive business plan to establish a clear brand identity and attract the right clients. A solid business plan should include the following components:

1. Executive Summary:

This brief overview highlights the mission, target audience, unique value proposition, and key objectives of the freelance business. It sets the tone for the rest of the document.

2. Business Description:

A detailed description of the freelance business, including its legal structure, services offered, target audience, and market positioning. It explains how the business stands out from competitors and why clients should choose it.

3. Market Analysis:

Thorough market research to understand the target market, industry trends, competition, and potential opportunities. Identifying the target audience's needs, pain points, and preferences helps identify a competitive advantage and develop effective strategies.

4. Marketing and Sales Strategy:

Outlining the marketing and sales approach to reach and attract clients. Defining brand identity, developing a marketing plan, and outlining strategies for promoting services through digital marketing, networking, referrals, or partnerships.

5. Service Offerings:

Describing core services in detail, including benefits, outcomes, features, and pricing. Consider packaging services into different tiers or packages to cater to different client needs and budgets. Clearly define what sets services apart from competitors.

6. Operational Plan:

Explaining how day-to-day operations will be managed, including setting up a home office or workspace, managing client communication and contracts, organizing finances, and utilizing productivity tools or software.

7. Financial Projections:

Creating projections that outline revenue streams, expected expenses, and profitability. Estimating income based on anticipated rates, project volume, or retainer clients. Including a budget for marketing expenses, professional development, and other business-related costs.

8. Pricing Strategy:

Defining pricing strategy based on factors such as market rates, industry standards, competition, and the value provided. Considering different pricing models (hourly rates, project-based fees) and how they align with the target audience's expectations.

9. Risk Assessment:

Identifying potential risks or challenges that could impact the freelance business, such as changes in market demand, economic factors, competition, or personal circumstances. Developing contingency plans to mitigate risks and ensure business continuity.

10. Implementation and Timeline:

Outlining the steps required to implement the business plan and setting realistic timelines for each milestone or objective. This helps freelancers stay organized and accountable as they work towards achieving their goals.

Regularly reviewing and updating the business plan as the freelance business evolves and market conditions change is essential. A solid business plan serves as a roadmap to guide decision-making and ensure the long-term success of the freelance venture.

Setting goals and creating a comprehensive business plan are crucial steps for freelancers to achieve success. By following practical tips for setting achievable goals and including essential components in a business plan, freelancers can establish a clear direction, attract the right clients, and position themselves as experts in their field. With clarity and focus, freelancers can navigate the freelance landscape with confidence and achieve their desired level of success.

CHAPTER 4

Crafting a Personal Brand

In the vast and ever-expanding world of freelancing, it can be challenging to stand out from the crowd. With countless freelancers offering similar services, how can you make a lasting impression on potential clients? The answer lies in crafting a strong personal brand.

A personal brand is more than just a logo or a catchy tagline. It is the essence of who you are as a freelancer, the unique value you bring to the table, and the reputation you build over time. In this chapter, we will explore the steps you can take to craft a personal brand that sets you apart from the competition and attracts the right clients.

Defining Your Niche

The first step in crafting a personal brand is to define your niche. What specific skills or services do you offer? Who is your target audience? Understanding your unique selling proposition will help you position yourself in the market. Take the time to identify your area of expertise and the audience you want to serve. This clarity will form the foundation of your personal brand.

Creating a Compelling Online Presence

Once you have defined your niche, it's time to build a compelling online presence. Your website is your virtual storefront, and it should showcase your portfolio, testimonials, and highlight your expertise. Optimize your website for search engines to increase visibility. Additionally, establish a strong presence on relevant social media platforms, such as LinkedIn or Instagram, to share your work and engage with your audience.

Developing Thought Leadership

Positioning yourself as an industry expert is a crucial aspect of crafting a personal brand. Share valuable insights through blog posts, articles, or even video content. This will help you build credibility and attract potential clients who are seeking your expertise. By consistently providing valuable content, you establish yourself as a trusted authority in your field.

Strategic Networking

Networking is an essential part of building a personal brand. Attend industry events, join online communities, and actively participate in relevant forums or groups. Networking allows you to connect with potential clients, collaborators, and mentors who can help enhance your personal brand. By building relationships and expanding your professional network, you increase your chances of finding new opportunities.

Leveraging Testimonials and Referrals

Positive reviews and referrals can greatly enhance your credibility and attract new clients. Request testimonials from satisfied clients and showcase them on your website or social media platforms. These testimonials serve as social proof and can significantly impact a potential client's decision to work with you. By leveraging testimonials and referrals, you build trust and establish yourself as a reliable and skilled freelancer.

Consistent Branding

Consistency is key when it comes to personal branding. Maintain a consistent visual identity across all your marketing materials, including your website, social media profiles, and business cards. Use consistent colors, fonts, and logos to create a cohesive brand image. This consistency helps create a memorable and professional impression on potential clients.

Engaging with Your Audience

Building a personal brand is not just about showcasing your work; it's also about engaging with your audience. Actively respond to comments, messages, and inquiries from potential clients or industry peers. Engaging with your audience helps build trust and establishes you as someone who values their connections. By actively participating in conversations and providing value, you foster relationships and create a loyal following.

Continuous Learning and Improvement

To stay ahead in the freelancing world, it's crucial to continuously learn and improve. Stay up-to-date with industry trends, technologies, and best practices. Invest in professional development opportunities like attending workshops or obtaining certifications to enhance your skills. By continuously learning and improving, you position yourself as a freelancer who is committed to delivering high-quality work and staying ahead of the competition.

Crafting a personal brand is an ongoing process. It requires time, effort, and a deep understanding of your strengths and target audience. By following these steps, freelancers can establish a strong personal brand that differentiates them from others in the market and attracts the right clients. Remember, your personal brand is not just about what you do; it's about who you are and the value you bring to the table. Embrace your uniqueness, showcase your expertise, and let your personal brand shine.

CHAPTER 5

Finding and Engaging Clients

In the world of freelancing, finding and engaging clients is essential for success. It is through these clients that freelancers can secure projects, build their reputation, and establish themselves as experts in their field. However, the process of finding and engaging clients can be challenging and requires a strategic approach. In this chapter, we will explore effective strategies for networking, utilizing freelancing platforms, leveraging referrals and testimonials, and avoiding common mistakes and pitfalls.

Networking: Building Relationships for Success

Networking is a crucial aspect of freelancing that can lead to valuable connections, referrals, and collaborations. To effectively network, freelancers should consider the following strategies:

1. Attend industry events:

By attending conferences, workshops, and meetups relevant to their industry, freelancers can meet potential clients, collaborators, and industry peers. Actively engage in conversations, exchange contact information, and be proactive in introducing yourself.

2. Join online communities:

Participating in online communities such as forums, LinkedIn groups, or Facebook groups allows freelancers to establish themselves as experts in their field and build relationships with like-minded professionals. Contribute valuable insights, answer questions, and initiate discussions.

3. Utilize social media:

Actively engage with your audience on social media platforms by following and interacting with influencers or industry leaders. Share valuable content and participate in relevant conversations. Connect with potential clients and peers through LinkedIn and engage with their posts or share insights.

4. Offer value and be helpful:

Networking is not just about taking but also giving. Offer assistance, provide valuable insights, or share resources without expecting anything in return. Being helpful builds trust and establishes you as someone others want to connect with.

5. Attend local business events:

Look for local networking events or meetups in your area. Engage in conversations, exchange business cards, and follow up with individuals you connect with to nurture the relationship.

6. Collaborate with other freelancers:

Seek out opportunities for collaboration with other freelancers who complement your skills or work in related fields. Collaborative projects not only expand your network but also allow you to tap into each other's client base and expertise.

7. Leverage existing connections:

Reach out to past clients, colleagues, or mentors and let them know about your freelance services. They may have referrals or recommendations that can help you kickstart your freelance career.

8. Follow up and maintain relationships:

After meeting new contacts or receiving referrals, make sure to follow up promptly. Send a personalized email or connect on

LinkedIn to express appreciation and continue the conversation. Stay in touch periodically by sharing relevant updates or resources to nurture the relationship.

By implementing these networking strategies consistently, freelancers can expand their professional network, increase visibility, and create valuable relationships that can contribute to their long-term success.

Utilizing Freelancing Platforms and Job Boards

Freelancing platforms and job boards can be valuable resources for freelancers to find and engage clients. To effectively utilize these platforms, freelancers should consider the following tips:

1. Choose the right platforms:

Research and identify the freelancing platforms and job boards that are most relevant to your industry and target audience. Consider factors such as the platform's reputation, user base, and the types of projects and clients available.

2. Optimize your profile:

Create a compelling profile that showcases your skills, experience, and portfolio. Highlight your unique selling points and use keywords relevant to your niche to increase visibility in search results. Include samples of your best work and testimonials from satisfied clients.

3. Customize proposals:

When applying for projects or gigs on freelancing platforms, take the time to craft personalized proposals. Tailor your proposals to each client's specific needs, demonstrating your understanding of their requirements and how you can provide value. Showcase relevant experience, skills, and examples of similar projects you have worked on.

4. Be proactive and responsive:

Actively search for relevant projects on the platform and submit proposals in a timely manner. Monitor responses and engage with potential clients promptly. Be professional, responsive, and provide any additional information or clarifications they may require.

5. Build a strong reputation:

Deliver high-quality work and provide exceptional customer service to clients you work with through freelancing platforms. Positive reviews and ratings can significantly enhance your reputation and attract more clients. Aim for long-term relationships with clients by exceeding their expectations.

6. Network within the platform:

Engage with other freelancers and potential clients within the platform's community features, such as forums or discussion boards. Participate in conversations, offer insights, and establish yourself as a helpful and knowledgeable professional.

7. Leverage feedback and ratings:

Request feedback from clients upon completion of projects and encourage them to leave positive reviews or ratings on the platform. These testimonials act as social proof and can influence potential clients' decision-making process.

8. Expand beyond the platform:

While freelancing platforms can be a great starting point, aim to build direct client relationships outside of these platforms as well. Use the projects you complete on the platform as case studies or examples to showcase your expertise on your own website or portfolio.

By effectively utilizing freelancing platforms and job boards, freelancers can find new clients, build their reputation, and grow their freelance business.

Leveraging Referrals and Testimonials

Referrals and testimonials play a vital role in establishing credibility as a freelancer. They provide social proof and demonstrate to potential clients that others have had positive experiences working with you. Here's how you can leverage referrals and testimonials effectively:

1. Request feedback:

Upon completing a project, proactively reach out to clients and ask for their feedback on your work. Ask them to provide specific details about what they appreciated most, how the project benefited them, or any unique aspects of your service that stood out.

2. Encourage testimonials:

Ask satisfied clients to provide written testimonials that highlight their positive experience working with you. These testimonials can be displayed on your website, social media profiles, or freelancing platform profiles. Make it easy for clients to provide testimonials by offering templates or guiding questions.

3. Showcase testimonials strategically:

Display testimonials prominently on your website or portfolio. Consider placing them on key pages such as the homepage, services page, or project showcase section. Use quotes or snippets from testimonials in marketing materials, social media posts, or email newsletters to reinforce your credibility.

4. Video testimonials:

If possible, request clients to provide video testimonials. Video testimonials are more engaging and authentic, and they can have a stronger impact on potential clients. You can embed these video testimonials on your website or share them on social media platforms.

5. Referral program:

Implement a referral program where you offer incentives or rewards to clients who refer new business to you. This encourages satisfied clients to actively recommend your services to their network, expanding your reach and credibility.

6. Case studies:

Develop detailed case studies that showcase specific projects you have worked on, the challenges you solved, and the results achieved for clients. Include client testimonials within the case studies to provide additional credibility and context.

7. LinkedIn recommendations:

Request recommendations from clients or colleagues on LinkedIn. These recommendations will appear on your LinkedIn profile and can be viewed by potential clients or collaborators. LinkedIn recommendations carry significant weight as they are tied to professional profiles.

8. Share success stories:

Share success stories or client testimonials as blog posts, articles, or social media content. Highlight the problem you solved for the client, the approach you took, and the positive impact it had on their business. This demonstrates your expertise and showcases the value you bring.

By leveraging referrals and testimonials effectively, freelancers can enhance their credibility, build trust with potential clients, and differentiate themselves from competitors.

Common Mistakes and Pitfalls to Avoid

When finding and engaging clients as a freelancer, there are common mistakes and pitfalls to avoid. These include:

1. Lack of focus:

Trying to be a generalist and targeting a broad range of clients can dilute your message and make it difficult to stand out. Instead, define your niche and target a specific audience. This allows you to position yourself as an expert and attract clients who value your specialized skills.

2. Neglecting online presence:

Having a strong online presence is crucial in today's digital age. Neglecting to build a professional website or maintain active profiles on relevant social media platforms can hinder your ability to attract clients. Make sure your online presence is up-to-date, showcases your work, and clearly communicates your value proposition.

3. Not defining clear boundaries:

Establishing clear boundaries with clients regarding project scope, deliverables, timelines, and payment terms is important. Failing to set these expectations upfront can lead to misunderstandings or scope creep, causing stress and potential conflicts down the line. Use well-written contracts or agreements to protect yourself and ensure a smooth client engagement.

4. Overpromising and underdelivering:

Promising the world to secure a client may seem tempting, but it's crucial to be realistic about what you can deliver. Overpromising and underdelivering can damage your reputation and lead to client dissatisfaction. Always set realistic expectations and strive to exceed them.

5. Poor communication:

Effective communication is key to successful client engagements. Lack of communication or poor responsiveness can lead to frustration and a breakdown in the working relationship. Be proactive in keeping clients informed of progress, responding promptly to their inquiries, and setting clear communication channels.

6. Failure to follow up:

Once a project is completed, it's important to follow up with clients for feedback or potential future opportunities. Neglecting to follow up can result in missed chances for repeat business or referrals. Stay in touch with past clients, nurture those relationships, and seek testimonials or referrals when appropriate.

7. Underestimating the power of referrals:

Referrals are a powerful source of new business for freelancers. Failing to ask for referrals or not nurturing relationships with existing clients or professional connections can mean missing out on valuable opportunities. Always remember to proactively ask satisfied clients for referrals and express gratitude when they make them.

By avoiding these common mistakes and pitfalls, freelancers can enhance their client engagement strategies, build stronger relationships, and increase their chances of long-term success in their freelance careers.

Finding and engaging clients as a freelancer is a crucial aspect of building a successful freelance business. By utilizing effective networking strategies, leveraging freelancing platforms, and leveraging referrals and testimonials, freelancers can attract new clients, build their reputation, and differentiate themselves from competitors. However, it's important to avoid common mistakes and pitfalls that can hinder client engagement. By implementing these strategies and avoiding pitfalls, freelancers can navigate the world of client engagement with confidence and set themselves up for long-term success.

CHAPTER 6

Pricing and Negotiating Contracts

As a freelancer, determining competitive rates for your services and negotiating fair compensation with clients are crucial aspects of building a successful freelance career. In this chapter, we will explore strategies for pricing your services effectively and negotiating contracts that ensure you are adequately compensated for your skills and expertise.

To determine competitive rates for your services, it is essential to consider several factors. First, conduct a thorough market analysis to understand the going rates for similar services in your industry and location. This can be done by researching online job boards, freelancer platforms, or networking with other professionals in the field. By understanding market standards, you can align your rates accordingly.

Next, assess your own skill level and expertise. Consider the value you bring to clients through higher levels of experience, specialized knowledge, or unique skills. These factors can justify higher rates and differentiate you from competitors. Additionally, take into account your cost of living and overhead expenses, such as software licenses, equipment, and marketing. Higher costs of living or significant overhead expenses may require higher rates to sustain profitability.

Estimating the time and effort required to complete a project is another important consideration. Projects that demand extensive research, multiple revisions, or tight deadlines may warrant higher rates. Lastly, identify your unique value proposition and how it differentiates you from competitors. If you can demonstrate that your services deliver exceptional value or solve a specific problem for clients, you can justify charging higher rates.

Once you have determined your competitive rates, it is time to negotiate with clients to ensure fair compensation. Effective negotiation strategies include conducting research and preparation beforehand, focusing on the value you provide rather than just the hours worked, presenting multiple pricing options, justifying your rates based on your skills and experience, being confident yet flexible, maintaining professionalism throughout the process, and documenting agreements once reached.

Research and preparation are essential to support your negotiation position. Understand industry standards, market rates, and the client's budget if possible. Prepare a clear understanding of your value proposition, the scope of work, and the benefits you bring to the client. During the negotiation, emphasize the value you provide and the positive impact your work will have on their business. Offer different pricing options or packages that align with their needs and budget, allowing them to choose the option that best suits their requirements. Justify your rates based on your skills, experience, and the value you bring. Share examples of past successful projects or client testimonials to demonstrate your capabilities. Be confident in your skills and value, but also be open to compromise and finding mutually beneficial solutions. Maintain professionalism and respect throughout the negotiation process, actively listening to the client's concerns and seeking common ground. Once an agreement is reached, document the terms and conditions in a clear contract or agreement.

Managing contract terms as a freelancer requires careful consideration of several key factors. Clearly define the scope of work in the contract to avoid any misunderstandings or scope creep. Specify deliverables, deadlines, and any additional services that may incur extra charges. Establish clear payment terms, including the payment schedule, accepted payment methods, and any late payment penalties or interest charges. Outline the ownership and usage rights of intellectual property in the contract, including any limitations or restrictions on its use. If the freelancer will have access to sensitive information or trade secrets, include a confidentiality or non-disclosure clause. Include provisions for contract termination, notice periods, and dispute resolution methods. Clearly define each party's responsibilities and liabilities in case of errors or damages. Consult with a legal professional experienced in contract law to ensure that your contract terms are legally sound and protect your interests.

To illustrate successful pricing and contract negotiation experiences, let me share a few examples from my own career. In one instance, a client required a complex website redesign that would significantly impact their online presence and user experience. Instead of charging by the hour, I presented a value-based pricing proposal that emphasized the potential increase in conversions and revenue that the new website could generate. By highlighting the value they would receive, I was able to negotiate a higher rate for the project.

In another example, I developed long-term relationships with clients, providing ongoing services such as content creation or social media management. In these cases, I negotiated retainer agreements where the client pays a fixed monthly fee for a set number of hours or deliverables. This arrangement ensures a steady income for me while offering clients priority access to my services.

Flexible payment terms can also be effective in negotiations for larger projects. By splitting the project cost into several milestones with payments tied to each milestone's completion, clients can manage their cash flow while ensuring regular payments throughout the project duration.

Additional services or add-ons can be included in contract

negotiations to provide more value to clients. For example, as a freelance writer, I might offer additional rounds of revisions or include proofreading and editing services at no extra cost. These add-ons increase the perceived value of my services and differentiate me from other freelancers.

Lastly, offering early payment discounts can incentivize prompt payment and build positive client relationships. By offering a discount for paying the invoice within a specified timeframe, clients are encouraged to pay quickly, ensuring a healthy cash flow for the freelancer.

To ensure fair compensation for your work and avoid undervaluing your services, there are several steps you can take. Research market rates to understand industry standards and align your rates accordingly. Assess your unique value proposition and communicate it effectively to clients. Consider your costs of living, business expenses, and the time required to complete projects. Set income goals based on your financial needs and desired lifestyle. Clearly define the scope of work and deliverables in your contracts to avoid scope creep. Track your time and effort to accurately assess the work you put in. Regularly reevaluate your rates to adjust for changes in market conditions, experience level, and demand for your services.

By implementing these strategies, freelancers can ensure fair compensation, maintain healthy client relationships, and build a successful freelance career. Pricing and negotiating contracts effectively are essential skills that contribute to long-term success and profitability.

CHAPTER 7

Financial Management for Freelancers

As a freelancer, managing your finances effectively is crucial for the success and sustainability of your business. In this chapter, we will explore the steps involved in setting up a separate business bank account, tracking income and expenses, tax considerations, budgeting strategies, and recommended financial management tools and resources. By implementing these practices, you can gain better control over your finances, make informed decisions, and ensure compliance with tax regulations.

Setting Up a Separate Business Bank Account:

Setting up a separate business bank account is the first step towards managing your finances as a freelancer. Research different banks and their business account offerings, considering factors such as fees, account features, online banking capabilities, customer service, and branch accessibility. Gather the required documents, such as your Social Security number or Employer Identification Number (EIN), proof of business registration or formation, and personal identification documents. Decide on the type of account that suits your needs, whether it's a business checking account, savings account, or a combination of both. Visit the bank or apply online, completing the application process and depositing the initial funds. Finally, set up online banking access and update your payment information with clients and financial platforms.

Tracking Income and Expenses:

To effectively track your income and expenses, it's essential to separate your business and personal finances. Open a dedicated business bank account to receive all business-related income and make business-related expenses. Choose a bookkeeping system that suits your needs, whether it's a simple spreadsheet or specialized accounting software. Record all income from clients or platforms, tracking invoices sent, payment dates, and amounts received. Consistently record all business-related expenses, categorizing them to gain insights into spending patterns. Automate processes by connecting your business bank account and credit cards to your bookkeeping system. Regularly reconcile your accounts and generate financial reports to gain insights into the financial health of your business. Consider consulting with an accountant or tax professional to ensure accurate tracking of income and expenses.

Tax Considerations:

Freelancers should be aware of their tax obligations and take steps to prepare for tax season effectively. Understand the tax obligations specific to your country and local jurisdiction. Keep track of income and expenses throughout the year, maintaining accurate records of invoices, receipts, bank statements, and other financial documents. Determine the appropriate tax filing status based on your business structure and consult with a tax professional if needed. Make estimated quarterly tax payments to cover your self-employment taxes and income tax liabilities. Familiarize yourself with deductible expenses applicable to your freelance business and organize all relevant documents needed for tax filing. Seek professional guidance from a tax professional or accountant to maximize deductions, ensure compliance with tax laws, and plan for tax liabilities. File taxes on time to avoid penalties and interest charges.

Budgeting Strategies:

Managing income fluctuations is a common challenge for freelancers. Create a monthly budget that reflects your average income and expenses, distinguishing between essential and non-essential expenses. Build an emergency fund to serve as a safety net during lean months or unexpected expenses. Smooth out income by setting up payment terms with clients that include regular, predictable payments. Track cash flow regularly, prioritize essential expenses, and adjust spending during high-income periods. Consider variable expenses and plan for taxes by setting aside a portion of each payment received. Diversify your client base to reduce reliance on a single client or industry. Continuously evaluate and adjust your budget based on changes in income, expenses, and financial goals.

Financial Management Tools and Resources:

There are several financial management tools and resources that can be helpful for freelancers. Utilize accounting software like QuickBooks, Xero, FreshBooks, or Wave for bookkeeping, expense tracking, invoicing, and generating financial reports. Consider using budgeting apps like Mint, YNAB, or PocketGuard to track income, expenses, and savings goals. Use receipt tracking apps such as Expensify or Shoeboxed to easily capture and categorize receipts for business expenses. Employ time-tracking tools to monitor the time spent on different client projects. Explore online payment platforms to facilitate easy and secure payment transactions with clients. Engage with personal finance blogs, tax resources, and professional associations to access valuable articles, tips, and resources tailored to freelancers.

Effectively managing your finances as a freelancer is essential for the success of your business. By setting up a separate business bank account, tracking income and expenses, understanding tax considerations, implementing budgeting strategies, and utilizing financial management tools and resources, you can gain better control over your finances, make informed decisions, and ensure compliance with tax regulations. Take the necessary steps to establish a solid financial foundation for your freelance business and pave the way for long-term financial success.

CHAPTER 8

Time Management and Productivity

Time management is a critical skill for freelancers to master in order to maximize productivity and maintain a healthy work-life balance. As a freelancer, the ability to effectively manage your time can make all the difference between success and burnout. In this chapter, we will explore various time management techniques and productivity strategies that can help freelancers optimize their workflow and achieve their goals.

Setting Clear Goals and Prioritizing:

One of the most effective time management techniques for freelancers is to set clear goals and prioritize tasks. By starting each day with a clear understanding of your objectives and identifying the most important tasks that align with those objectives, you can stay focused and ensure that you prioritize tasks that have the greatest impact on your business. This approach allows you to work towards your goals in a structured and purposeful manner.

Creating a Schedule:

Establishing a schedule is another crucial aspect of effective time management. By outlining your work hours and breaks, you can create a structured routine that helps you stay disciplined and allocate dedicated time for different tasks and projects. Having a schedule also allows you to manage client expectations regarding your availability and helps you maintain a healthy work-life balance.

Breaking Tasks into Manageable Chunks:

Large projects can often feel overwhelming, making it difficult to know where to start. To combat this, it is helpful to break down larger projects into smaller, more manageable tasks. This approach allows you to tackle tasks more effectively and gives you a sense of progress as you complete each smaller task. By breaking tasks into manageable chunks, you can maintain momentum and avoid feeling overwhelmed.

Utilizing Time-Blocking Techniques:

Time-blocking is a powerful technique that involves allocating specific time slots for different activities or tasks. By visually blocking out time for specific work, such as client meetings, project work, or administrative tasks, you can better manage your time and stay on track. Time-blocking helps you allocate dedicated focus to each task and minimizes the risk of getting sidetracked or overwhelmed by competing priorities.

Practicing the Pomodoro Technique:

The Pomodoro Technique is a popular time management technique that can help freelancers maintain focus and productivity. This technique involves setting a timer for 25 minutes of concentrated work, followed by a short 5-minute break. After completing four Pomodoros, a longer break is taken to recharge. By working in focused bursts and incorporating regular breaks, you can maintain high levels of concentration and productivity throughout the day.

Minimizing Distractions:

Distractions can significantly impact productivity, so it is important for freelancers to be conscious of minimizing them. Turning off notifications on your phone and computer, creating a dedicated workspace free from distractions, and using website blockers to limit access to distracting websites during work hours are all effective strategies for minimizing distractions. By creating a focused work environment, you can optimize your productivity and stay on task.

Delegating or Outsourcing:

As a freelancer, it is essential to recognize when to delegate or outsource tasks that can be handled by others. By doing so, you can focus on higher-value activities that align with your expertise and business goals. Delegating or outsourcing tasks such as administrative work or certain aspects of projects allows you to optimize your time and ensure that your efforts are focused on tasks that have the greatest impact on your business.

Practicing Time Batching:

Time batching involves grouping similar tasks together and scheduling specific time blocks for them. For example, you can dedicate specific time slots for email management, client communication, or content creation. This approach minimizes context switching and improves efficiency by allowing you to focus on specific types of tasks during dedicated time periods. Time batching helps you maintain focus and productivity by reducing the need to constantly switch between different types of tasks.

Regularly Assessing and Reflecting:

Taking regular breaks to assess your productivity and reflect on what is working well and what needs improvement is crucial for optimizing your time management and productivity. This self-reflection allows you to identify any time-wasting habits or inefficiencies and make necessary adjustments. By regularly assessing and reflecting on your work, you can continuously improve your time management skills and maximize your productivity.

Taking Breaks and Resting:

Prioritizing self-care is essential for maintaining productivity and preventing burnout as a freelancer. Taking regular breaks and ensuring that you get enough rest is crucial for maintaining focus, creativity, and overall productivity. By prioritizing self-care, you can recharge and rejuvenate, allowing you to bring your best self to your work.

Effective time management is the key to maximizing productivity and maintaining a healthy work-life balance as a freelancer. By implementing the time management techniques and productivity strategies discussed in this chapter, you can optimize your workflow, achieve your goals, and thrive in your freelance career. Remember that time management is an ongoing process that requires consistent effort and self-awareness. By prioritizing your tasks effectively and managing your time wisely, you can unlock your full potential as a freelancer and achieve success on your own terms.

CHAPTER 9

Scaling Your Freelance Business

Scaling a freelance business is an exciting but challenging endeavor. As freelancers experience growth and increased demand for their services, they may find themselves faced with the need to expand their operations. This chapter explores the considerations, strategies, and pitfalls associated with scaling a freelance business. From hiring subcontractors to implementing streamlined processes and investing in professional development, freelancers can navigate the path to growth and success.

The Need for Scaling:

Freelancers may consider scaling their business under various circumstances. One of the primary reasons is an increased workload. When the volume of work exceeds the freelancer's capacity, hiring subcontractors or building a team becomes essential. This could be due to an increase in client projects, larger-scale projects, or a desire to take on more clients without compromising quality or delivery times.

Another reason to scale is specialized skills or expertise. When faced with projects that require skills outside of their core competencies, freelancers can hire subcontractors or team members with the necessary expertise. This allows them to offer a broader range of services and take on more diverse projects.

Time constraints can also drive the need for scaling. If freelancers find it challenging to complete projects within desired deadlines, additional support in the form of subcontractors or team members can help meet project timelines. This is particularly relevant when dealing with multiple simultaneous projects or projects with tight deadlines.

Scalability and growth are also significant factors. By hiring subcontractors or building a team, freelancers can focus on higher-value activities, business development, and strategic planning. This can lead to increased revenue, expanded service offerings, and the ability to take on larger or more complex projects.

Strategies for Scaling:

To scale their freelance business effectively, freelancers need to implement streamlined systems and processes. These systems and processes ensure efficient operations and support sustainable growth. Some key strategies to consider include:

1. Client Onboarding:

Develop a standardized client onboarding process to ensure a smooth transition from initial contact to project initiation. This includes creating welcome packets, outlining project requirements, setting expectations, and establishing clear communication channels.

2. Project Management:

Utilize project management tools or software to streamline project workflows, assign tasks, track progress, and manage deadlines. This helps ensure that projects stay on track, team members are aligned, and client expectations are met.

3. Time Tracking and Invoicing:

Implement a time tracking system to accurately record billable hours for client projects. This can help streamline invoicing and ensure prompt and accurate billing. Integrate it with accounting or invoicing software for seamless financial management.

4. Communication and Collaboration:

Use communication and collaboration tools to facilitate effective communication with clients and team members. Platforms like Slack, Trello, or Microsoft Teams enable real-time communication, file sharing, and task management, fostering collaboration and streamlining workflows.

5. File Management:

Establish a well-organized file management system to store and retrieve project files efficiently. Cloud storage platforms like Google Drive or Dropbox offer secure and accessible storage options for documents, designs, or other project-related files.

6. Standardized Templates:

Develop standardized templates for proposals, contracts, invoices, and other recurring documents to save time and maintain consistency in communications. Customizable templates can be created using word processing or invoicing software.

7. Financial Management:

Set up systems for financial management, including bookkeeping, expense tracking, and tax preparation. Accounting software like QuickBooks or Xero can help streamline financial processes, generate reports, and simplify tax-related tasks.

8. Client Relationship Management (CRM):

Implement a CRM system to manage client relationships, track leads, and monitor client interactions. CRM tools like HubSpot or Salesforce organize client data, allow for personalized communication, and help nurture long-term client relationships.

9. Quality Assurance:

Establish quality assurance processes to review and ensure the accuracy, completeness, and consistency of deliverables before final submission to clients. This may involve proofreading, testing, or peer review procedures.

10. Continuous Improvement:

Regularly evaluate systems and processes to identify areas for improvement. Seek feedback from clients and team members to refine operations and make adjustments as needed.

Investing in Professional Development:

As client demands evolve, freelancers must invest in professional development to stay competitive. Continual learning is crucial for staying updated on industry trends, new technologies, and best practices. Attending conferences, workshops, webinars, or online courses can enhance skills and broaden knowledge.

Networking and collaboration are also valuable for professional growth. Engaging with other professionals in the industry through industry-specific groups, meetups, and events can provide opportunities for skill-sharing and collaborative projects. Seeking out mentors or coaches can offer guidance and support based on their experience.

Thought leadership and content creation are effective ways to showcase expertise and attract clients. Sharing insights through blog posts, articles, or video tutorials establishes freelancers as knowledgeable resources in their field.

Challenges and Pitfalls:

Scaling a freelance business comes with its fair share of challenges and pitfalls. Some common ones include:

1. Capacity and Workload Management:

As freelancers take on more clients or larger projects, managing capacity and workload becomes challenging. Prioritizing tasks, delegating or outsourcing, and setting clear boundaries with clients can help overcome this challenge.

2. Client Communication and Expectations:

Effectively managing client communication and expectations becomes crucial when scaling a business. Setting clear expectations, communicating regularly, and using project management tools can help overcome this challenge.

3. Scaling Pricing and Rates:

Determining appropriate pricing and rates when scaling a freelance business can be challenging. Researching market rates, considering value-based pricing, and regularly reviewing pricing structures can help overcome this challenge.

4. Hiring and Managing a Team or Subcontractors:

When scaling, freelancers may need to hire team members or subcontractors. Clearly defining roles and responsibilities, implementing effective communication tools, and providing proper training and support can overcome the challenges of managing a team.

5. Maintaining Quality and Consistency:

Scaling a business while maintaining quality and consistency can be a challenge. Developing standardized processes, regularly evaluating work quality, and investing in ongoing professional development can help overcome this challenge.

6. Financial Management:

Scaling a freelance business requires effective financial management. Implementing accounting software, setting aside funds for taxes and emergencies, and regularly reviewing financial performance can help overcome financial challenges.

Successful Examples:

Several successful freelancers have scaled their businesses and experienced significant career impacts. For example:

1. Jane, a freelance graphic designer, scaled her business by expanding her service offerings to include website design and branding. This allowed her to attract larger clients, increase revenue, and establish herself as a reputable expert.

2. Mark, a freelance writer, built a team of content writers and editors, allowing him to handle a higher volume of projects and secure contracts from various industries. This led to significant growth in revenue and client referrals.

3. Sarah, a freelance digital marketer, specialized in social media marketing for small businesses. By positioning herself as an expert in this niche, she attracted clients seeking her expertise, resulting in higher rates and long-term client relationships.

4. David, a freelance photographer, invested in professional equipment and expanded his services to include event photography and videography. Hiring additional photographers and videographers allowed him to handle larger projects, secure contracts for major events, and increase revenue significantly.

Scaling a freelance business requires careful planning, effective systems and processes, and continuous professional development. By implementing streamlined operations, investing in professional growth, and overcoming common challenges, freelancers can achieve sustainable growth and success in the freelance industry. With the right strategies and mindset, freelancers can turn their side hustle into a thriving full-time gig.

CHAPTER 10

Overcoming Challenges and Building Resilience

In the world of freelancing, challenges are inevitable. From irregular income to client acquisition, time management to self-motivation, freelancers face a myriad of obstacles that can hinder their success. However, by implementing effective strategies and developing resilience, freelancers can navigate these challenges and build a thriving freelance career.

One common challenge that freelancers face is irregular income. The unpredictability of freelance work often leads to inconsistent paychecks. To overcome this challenge, freelancers should establish a budget and save for lean periods. By setting aside funds during prosperous times, freelancers can weather the storm during slower periods. Diversifying their client base is another strategy to reduce reliance on a single source of income. By expanding their network and seeking out new clients, freelancers can create a more stable income stream. Setting clear payment terms and following up on late payments is also crucial. By establishing expectations upfront and being proactive in collecting payments, freelancers can ensure a steady cash flow. Additionally, offering retainer agreements or recurring revenue streams can provide a consistent source of income.

Another significant challenge for freelancers is client acquisition. Finding and securing clients can be a daunting task. To overcome this challenge, freelancers should focus on developing a strong online presence. This can be achieved through a professional website, an impressive portfolio, and active engagement on social media. By showcasing their skills and expertise online, freelancers can attract potential clients. Networking and building relationships with industry professionals is also essential. Attending industry events, joining online communities, and seeking referrals can lead to valuable connections and collaborative opportunities. Providing exceptional service to existing clients is another strategy for client acquisition. By exceeding expectations and delivering high-quality work, freelancers can encourage word-of-mouth recommendations and attract new clients. Collaborating with other freelancers or agencies can also expand a freelancer's client base and open doors to new opportunities.

Time management is another challenge that freelancers often face. With no set schedule or supervisor, freelancers must take responsibility for managing their time effectively. To overcome this challenge, freelancers should set clear goals and prioritize tasks based on importance and deadlines. Utilizing productivity techniques such as time blocking or the Pomodoro Technique can help freelancers stay focused and maximize their productivity. Task management tools and calendars can also assist in staying organized and tracking progress. Minimizing distractions and establishing boundaries is crucial for maintaining focus. By creating a dedicated workspace and setting boundaries between work and personal life, freelancers can optimize their productivity.

Self-motivation and discipline are essential qualities for freelancers. Without the structure of a traditional work environment, freelancers must stay motivated and disciplined in managing their work. Setting specific goals and breaking them down into actionable steps is a strategy for staying motivated. By having a clear vision of what they want to achieve, freelancers can stay focused and driven. Establishing a routine and sticking to it is another way to create structure in the workday. By following a consistent schedule, freelancers can maintain discipline and avoid procrastination. Finding accountability partners or joining communities of freelancers can provide support and motivation. Celebrating achievements and rewarding oneself for meeting milestones can also boost motivation and maintain a positive mindset.

Skill development is crucial for freelancers to stay competitive in their field. To overcome the challenge of continuously updating their skills, freelancers should invest in ongoing learning. This can be achieved through courses, workshops, or online resources. Joining professional associations or communities can provide access to industry insights and networking opportunities. Seeking feedback from clients and actively working on improving skills based on their input is another strategy for skill development. Collaborating with other freelancers to learn from their expertise and expand knowledge is also beneficial.

Work-life balance is a challenge that freelancers often struggle with. Balancing work and personal life can be difficult when working from home. To overcome this challenge, freelancers should set boundaries between work and personal time. Establishing dedicated work hours and creating a separate workspace can help separate work from home life. Prioritizing self-care, scheduling breaks, and making time for hobbies or activities outside of work is crucial for maintaining a healthy work-life balance. Delegating or outsourcing non-essential tasks can also free up time for personal pursuits.

In order to navigate these challenges and achieve success, freelancers must develop resilience and a growth mindset. Continuous learning is a key strategy for developing resilience. By engaging in ongoing learning and development, freelancers can acquire new skills and knowledge that will help them handle challenges and adapt to changing market demands. Networking and collaboration are also important for resilience. By building relationships with peers, freelancers can share experiences, exchange ideas, and gain support during challenging times. Collaborative projects can lead to new opportunities and diversify their client base. Goal setting and planning are essential for resilience. By setting clear goals and creating a strategic plan, freelancers can track their progress and stay motivated. Embracing failure as a learning opportunity is another strategy for building resilience. By reframing failures as valuable experiences, freelancers can extract lessons learned and apply them to future challenges. Building a support system and maintaining a positive mindset are also crucial for resilience. Surrounding oneself with mentors, coaches, or industry experts who can provide guidance and support is essential. Cultivating a positive mindset through self-care, setting boundaries, and managing stress levels can help freelancers approach challenges with clarity and resilience.

Freelancers can learn valuable lessons from failures and use them as opportunities for growth. Failures can highlight specific areas where freelancers need to improve their skills, knowledge, or processes. By reflecting on the reasons behind the failure, freelancers can identify gaps and take proactive steps to address them. Adapting and pivoting is another strategy for growth. Failures often indicate that freelancers need to adjust their approach or pivot their business strategy. By analyzing the reasons behind the failure, freelancers can make necessary changes to overcome challenges and seize new opportunities. Building resilience is crucial for growth. By embracing failure as a learning experience and reframing it as a temporary setback, freelancers can bounce back stronger. Seeking feedback and learning from mistakes is another strategy for growth. By actively seeking feedback and being open to criticism, freelancers can continuously enhance their skills and deliver better results. Embracing a growth mindset is essential for growth. By adopting a mindset that abilities and intelligence can be developed through dedication and hard work, freelancers can view failures as opportunities for growth and challenges as chances to learn and improve.

Personal experiences and examples of freelancers who have overcome challenges and achieved success serve as inspiration for others. One example is a graphic designer who faced a significant setback when a major client ended their contract. Instead of letting this loss of income defeat them, the designer used it as an opportunity to diversify their client base. They reached out to existing clients to offer additional services and explored new industries where their design skills could be utilized. By networking and collaborating with other freelancers, they discovered new opportunities for partnerships and referrals. They also invested time in improving their skills through online courses. Through perseverance and adaptability, this graphic designer not only replaced the lost client but also expanded their client base and increased their income significantly.

Another inspiring example is a freelance writer who faced a period of low demand for their services. Instead of becoming discouraged, they focused on building their personal brand by consistently publishing valuable content on their blog and guest posting on industry-leading websites. This strategic effort helped them establish themselves as an authority in their niche and attracted new clients seeking their expertise. They actively sought feedback from clients and continuously honed their writing skills based on the constructive criticism they received. By leveraging social media platforms to showcase their portfolio and engage with potential clients, they secured long-term retainer contracts with high-profile clients.

These examples highlight the importance of resilience, adaptability, continuous learning, networking, and strategic marketing efforts in overcoming challenges. By embracing these strategies, freelancers can navigate setbacks and position themselves for long-term success in their respective industries.

Staying motivated and focused during challenging times is crucial for freelancers. Setting clear goals, creating a routine, finding inspiration, celebrating small wins, seeking support, taking breaks, practicing self-care, and continuously learning and growing are strategies that can help freelancers maintain their motivation and focus. By implementing these strategies, freelancers can overcome challenges and achieve their goals.

Freelancers face various challenges on their journey to success. However, by implementing effective strategies, developing resilience, and maintaining a growth mindset, freelancers can overcome these challenges and build a thriving freelance career. Through continuous learning, networking, goal setting, embracing failure, building a support system, and maintaining a positive mindset, freelancers can navigate setbacks and seize opportunities for growth. By staying motivated, focused, and adaptable, freelancers can overcome challenges and achieve their goals in the ever-evolving world of freelancing.

CHAPTER 11

Transitioning to Full-Time Freelancing

The leap from a side hustle to full-time freelancing can be both exciting and daunting. As a freelancer, you have the freedom to work on your own terms and pursue your passions, but there are also financial considerations and fears that may arise during this transition. In this chapter, we will explore the steps you can take to ensure a smooth and successful transition to full-time freelancing, as well as address common misconceptions and fears that freelancers may have.

Before making the leap, it is crucial to create a financial plan that assesses your current financial situation and outlines your monthly expenses. This plan should include rent or mortgage payments, utilities, insurance, groceries, transportation, and debt obligations. Understanding your financial obligations will help you determine how much income you need to generate as a freelancer to cover your expenses. Additionally, building an emergency fund that can cover at least three to six months of living expenses is essential. This fund will act as a safety net during lean periods or unexpected circumstances.

Estimating your income and setting rates is another crucial step in the transition process. Determine how much income you need to earn as a freelancer to meet your financial goals. Research industry rates and consider factors such as your experience, expertise, and market demand when setting your freelance rates. Be realistic about the number of billable hours you can achieve each month and consider any non-billable time for marketing, administrative tasks, and personal development.

Tracking expenses and maintaining budget discipline is vital for freelancers. Keep a record of all business-related expenses, such as equipment, software, marketing, professional development, and workspace costs. This will help you manage your cash flow effectively and ensure you are maximizing deductible expenses when filing taxes. It is also important to secure health insurance coverage independently as freelancers do not have employer-provided benefits. Explore options such as private insurance plans or joining professional associations that offer group coverage. Additionally, consider setting up retirement accounts like IRAs or Solo 401(k)s to save for the future.

Establishing clear invoicing and payment terms with clients is crucial for maintaining a steady cash flow. Clearly communicate your payment expectations, including due dates and late payment penalties if applicable. Consider using online invoicing tools or platforms that automate the process and provide reminders for outstanding payments. Familiarize yourself with tax obligations specific to freelancers in your country or region and consider consulting with a tax professional or accountant for guidance on tax planning, deductions, and compliance.

Once you have addressed the financial considerations, it is time to focus on marketing strategies to sustain a full-time income. Start by defining your target audience and understanding their needs, pain points, and preferences. This will allow you to tailor your marketing efforts to reach the right clients who are most likely to hire your services. Building a strong personal brand is also crucial. Clearly communicate your unique value proposition, showcase your expertise, and highlight your track record of delivering high-quality work. Consistently maintain your brand across all marketing channels, including your website, social media profiles, and portfolio.

Investing in a professional website that showcases your portfolio, services, testimonials, and contact information is essential.

Optimize your website for search engines to increase its visibility and ensure it is mobile-friendly for easy access on different devices. Regularly update your website with fresh content, such as blog posts or case studies, to demonstrate your expertise and engage potential clients. Leverage social media platforms strategically to connect with your target audience, establish thought leadership, and generate leads. Identify the platforms where your audience is most active and create engaging content that resonates with them.

Networking and collaboration are also key to sustaining a full-time income. Actively network with professionals in your industry and related fields to expand your reach and generate referrals. Attend industry conferences, join online communities, and participate in networking events where you can connect with potential clients or collaborators. Collaborating with other freelancers or agencies can lead to joint projects and shared referrals.

Content marketing is another effective strategy for attracting clients. Share valuable content through various channels to position yourself as an authority in your field and attract clients. Write informative blog posts, create video tutorials, or host webinars that address common challenges faced by your target audience. Share this content on your website, social media platforms, or guest post on industry-relevant websites to reach a wider audience.

Client testimonials and case studies are powerful tools for building trust and attracting new clients. Request testimonials from satisfied clients and showcase them on your website or marketing materials. Additionally, create case studies that highlight successful projects you have completed, showcasing the value you delivered to clients.

Email marketing is a valuable strategy for staying top-of-mind with your audience. Build an email list of potential clients and interested prospects by offering valuable content or resources in exchange for their email addresses. Regularly send newsletters or updates containing useful information, industry insights, or special offers to stay connected with your audience.

Continuous professional development is crucial for staying competitive in the freelance industry. Invest in acquiring new skills or certifications and share updates about your professional development. This demonstrates your commitment to staying relevant in your field and positions you as an expert who can provide up-to-date solutions to clients' problems.

Implementing a referral program can also help you expand your client base. Incentivize existing clients or contacts to refer new clients to you by offering rewards such as discounts on future services or other valuable incentives.

While transitioning to full-time freelancing, freelancers may have certain misconceptions or fears that can hold them back. Common misconceptions include the fear of lack of stable income, difficulty in finding clients, setting the right rates, feeling isolated, and lacking job security. These fears can be addressed by creating a financial plan, diversifying your client base, investing in marketing efforts, networking, setting realistic expectations, and continuously investing in professional development.

To ensure a smooth and successful transition to full-time freelancing, freelancers should plan and prepare by creating a detailed plan, securing clients and projects, setting realistic expectations, establishing a solid online presence, developing a strong personal brand, networking and collaborating, prioritizing professional development, setting clear policies and contracts, managing finances effectively, and seeking support from fellow freelancers and industry professionals.

By taking these steps and addressing common fears and misconceptions, freelancers can confidently transition to full-time freelancing and achieve their income goals. The journey may have its challenges, but with careful planning, perseverance, and a commitment to continuous improvement, freelancers can thrive in their freelance careers.

CHAPTER 12
Building a Support Network

In the vast world of freelancing, it can often feel like you're on your own. The solitude of working independently can bring about unique challenges and uncertainties. That's why building a support network is crucial for freelancers. It provides emotional support, knowledge sharing, collaboration opportunities, referrals, and networking connections that contribute to their success and well-being.

First and foremost, a support network offers emotional support. Freelancing can be a solitary profession, and the lack of social interaction can lead to feelings of isolation. By connecting with like-minded individuals who understand your experiences, you can find a sense of community. This support network can help alleviate the loneliness, boost your motivation, and provide encouragement during challenging times.

Furthermore, building a support network allows freelancers to tap into the collective knowledge and experience of others in their field. By learning from each other's successes and failures, sharing best practices, and exchanging valuable insights, freelancers can stay updated with industry trends, enhance their skills, and gain new perspectives on their work. It's a continuous learning process that helps freelancers grow and evolve in their careers.

Collaboration opportunities are another benefit of having a support network. By connecting with other freelancers or professionals in complementary fields, freelancers can expand the range of services they offer. Collaborating on projects not only leads to shared referrals and increased exposure but also allows freelancers to deliver more comprehensive solutions to clients. By tapping into the expertise of others, freelancers can enhance their value proposition and stand out in the competitive freelancing market.

Referrals and networking are also facilitated by a strong support network. When freelancers build relationships with peers who have complementary skills or work in related industries, they can refer clients to each other when their expertise is needed. Additionally, networking within the support network can lead to new opportunities, partnerships, and collaborations. It's a way to expand your client base and open doors to exciting ventures.

So, how can freelancers go about building a support network? There are several steps they can take:

1. Join online communities:

Seek out online communities or forums where freelancers gather to connect, share experiences, and seek advice. Actively participate by engaging in discussions, asking questions, and offering insights. Platforms like LinkedIn groups, Facebook groups, or industry-specific forums are great places to start.

2. Attend industry events:

Conferences, workshops, webinars, or local meetups relevant to your field or industry provide opportunities to meet fellow freelancers, industry leaders, and potential clients. Engage in conversations, exchange contact information, and follow up with connections afterward.

3. Reach out to peers:

Proactively reach out to other freelancers in your field or related fields. Connect through social media platforms like LinkedIn or Twitter and initiate conversations. Offer help or advice when you can and be open to receiving support in return.

4. Seek mentorship:

Identify experienced freelancers or industry professionals who you admire and respect. Reach out to them for mentorship or guidance. Many successful freelancers are willing to share their knowledge and offer support to those starting out in the field.

5. Engage in local networking:

Attend local business networking events or join professional associations relevant to your field. These events provide opportunities to meet other professionals, potential clients, and industry leaders in your area.

By actively engaging in these activities and nurturing relationships over time, freelancers can build a strong support network that provides emotional support, knowledge sharing, collaboration opportunities, referrals, and networking connections. It's an investment in their success and well-being as freelancers.

Personal experiences and examples can shed light on how a support network has benefited freelancers in their careers. For instance, as a freelancer myself, I have experienced the advantages firsthand. Building connections within my support network has provided me with opportunities to learn from others, collaborate on projects, receive referrals, and find emotional support during challenging times.

One example is when I joined an online community of freelancers in my niche. Through interactions with these freelancers, I learned about a new software tool that significantly improved my productivity. The support network enabled me to stay updated and enhance my skills, giving me a competitive edge in the market.

Collaboration has also been a significant benefit of my support network. I connected with a graphic designer through a networking event, and we collaborated on several projects, offering our services as a package deal to clients seeking both design and development work. This collaboration led to successful projects and referrals from satisfied clients who appreciated our seamless partnership.

Moreover, the emotional support and encouragement from my support network have been invaluable. During moments of setback or discouragement, reaching out to fellow freelancers for advice and reassurance has helped me regain confidence and motivation. Knowing that I'm not alone in facing challenges as a freelancer has made a significant difference in how I approach future obstacles.

To leverage their support network, freelancers can seek advice and guidance from fellow freelancers when facing challenges or uncertainties. Sharing knowledge, insights, and resources within the network establishes them as valuable members and may lead to new opportunities. Collaborating on projects with other freelancers or professionals expands their portfolio and opens doors to joint marketing efforts and shared referrals. Referrals and recommendations from the support network can also be a valuable source of new business opportunities. Finally, the emotional support and motivation from the network can help freelancers navigate the ups and downs of freelancing with resilience.

Building a support network is crucial for freelancers. It provides emotional support, knowledge sharing, collaboration opportunities, referrals, and networking connections that contribute to their success and well-being. By actively engaging in activities like joining online communities, attending industry events, reaching out to peers, seeking mentorship, and engaging in local networking, freelancers can build a strong support network that enhances their career growth and provides the necessary support to thrive in the freelance world.

CHAPTER 13

Continuous Learning and Professional Development

In the ever-evolving world of freelancing, continuous learning is not just important, but crucial for success. As industries and markets rapidly change, freelancers need to stay updated with the latest trends, technologies, and best practices to remain relevant and competitive. Continuous learning allows freelancers to enhance their skills, expand their service offerings, and adapt to changing client needs. It also provides personal growth and satisfaction, allowing freelancers to challenge themselves, explore new areas of interest, and find inspiration for their work.

To prioritize professional development, freelancers need to allocate dedicated time in their schedule for learning activities. It should be treated as an essential part of their work routine rather than an afterthought. By setting aside specific hours or days each week or month for continuous learning, freelancers can ensure they make progress towards their learning objectives.

Identifying areas for improvement is also crucial in prioritizing professional development. Reflecting on strengths and weaknesses and seeking feedback from clients or peers can help freelancers identify areas where they want to improve or acquire new skills. This self-awareness is the first step in the journey of continuous learning.

Freelancers can find a plethora of resources and opportunities for professional development. Online learning platforms like Udemy, Coursera, LinkedIn Learning, and Skillshare offer a wide range of courses and tutorials on various topics. These platforms allow freelancers to learn new skills, enhance existing ones, and gain industry-specific knowledge. Webinars and virtual workshops offered by organizations, industry experts, and professional associations are also great opportunities for learning. By participating in these virtual events, freelancers can learn from experienced professionals, gain insights into emerging trends, and acquire new skills.

Following industry-specific publications, blogs, and newsletters is another effective way for freelancers to stay updated with industry trends. Subscribing to these sources and regularly reading articles, case studies, and thought leadership pieces can keep freelancers informed about the happenings in their field. Joining professional associations and organizations related to their industry is also beneficial for freelancers. These associations often provide resources, webinars, workshops, conferences, and networking events that aid in professional development.

Engaging in online communities, forums, and social media groups dedicated to freelancers or professionals in their industry is a valuable source of information and learning. Platforms like Reddit, LinkedIn Groups, Facebook Groups, or specialized forums provide spaces for knowledge sharing, discussions, and opportunities for professional growth. Actively participating in these communities allows freelancers to learn from others and share their own insights.

While balancing workload and making time for continuous learning can be challenging, it is not impossible. Freelancers can schedule dedicated time for learning, prioritize their learning goals, and set specific objectives. Embracing the concept of microlearning and utilizing smaller pockets of time throughout the day can also be effective. Blending learning with work by researching and exploring new techniques or tools while working on relevant tasks allows freelancers to learn while being productive. Automation and streamlining of tasks can free up more time for learning and development activities.

The impact of continuous learning on freelancers' careers cannot be overstated. It expands their skill set, allows them to adapt to industry changes, enhances client satisfaction, leverages new opportunities, builds confidence, and fosters valuable professional relationships. Continuous learning is a long-term commitment that requires intentional time management and utilization of available resources. By striking a balance between client work and professional development, freelancers can ensure they stay competitive, provide high-quality services, adapt to client needs, and experience personal growth in their freelance careers.

In the fast-paced world of freelancing, continuous learning is not just a luxury; it is a necessity. It is the key to staying relevant, adapting to industry changes, and remaining competitive. By prioritizing professional development and making it an ongoing commitment, freelancers can ensure they stay ahead of the curve, provide exceptional services, and achieve success in their freelance careers. So, embrace the journey of continuous learning, expand your horizons, and watch your freelance business thrive.

CHAPTER 14

Managing Client Relationships

Building and maintaining strong client relationships is essential for freelancers to thrive in their careers. Effective communication, handling difficult clients, securing repeat business, and ensuring client satisfaction are all key elements in managing client relationships successfully. In this chapter, we will explore strategies and personal experiences that will help freelancers navigate the complexities of client relationships and achieve long-term success.

Effective Communication Strategies

Effective communication is the foundation of any successful client relationship. By implementing clear and timely communication, active listening, setting realistic expectations, using clear and professional language, and providing regular progress updates, freelancers can establish trust, transparency, and collaboration with their clients. These strategies not only manage client expectations but also contribute to client satisfaction, repeat business, and positive referrals.

Handling Difficult Clients and Conflict Resolution

Difficult clients and conflicts are inevitable in any professional setting. Freelancers must remain calm and professional, practice active listening and empathy, seek clarification and provide explanations, offer solutions, document agreements and changes, set boundaries, involve a third party if necessary, and learn from the experience. By handling difficult clients and conflicts in a professional manner, freelancers can preserve client relationships and maintain their reputation as reliable professionals.

Building Long-Term Relationships and Securing Repeat Business

Building long-term relationships with clients and securing repeat business requires excellent customer service, consistent delivery of quality products or services, and continuous communication. By understanding clients' needs, providing exceptional customer service, maintaining consistent quality, fostering open communication, offering incentives for loyalty, building a strong after-sales support system, and developing long-term partnerships, freelancers can create a foundation for long-term success and growth in their freelance careers.

Personal Experiences and Examples

Personal experiences and examples play a crucial role in understanding the impact of successful client relationships on freelancers' careers. Through client referrals and retaining long-term clients, freelancers can expand their network, generate more business opportunities, secure a steady stream of work, gain valuable experience and knowledge within specific industries, and achieve financial stability. By consistently delivering quality work, providing excellent customer service, and nurturing client relationships, freelancers can unlock new opportunities for career growth and professional development.

Managing client relationships is a multifaceted process that requires effective communication, conflict resolution, and the ability to secure repeat business. By implementing the strategies discussed in this chapter and drawing from personal experiences, freelancers can establish strong client relationships, maintain client satisfaction, and achieve long-term success in their freelance careers. The key lies in understanding clients' needs, providing exceptional service, delivering consistent quality, and fostering open and transparent communication. With these skills, freelancers can thrive in their chosen field and build a reputation as reliable and trusted professionals.

CHAPTER 15

Marketing Beyond Online Platforms

In the fast-paced world of freelancing, it's easy to get caught up in the digital realm. Online platforms offer convenience and reach, but they shouldn't be the sole focus of your marketing efforts. To truly stand out and attract potential clients, freelancers must explore offline marketing strategies that go beyond the virtual sphere. In this chapter, we will delve into the power of networking, public speaking, and other thought leadership opportunities to enhance your marketing efforts and propel your freelance career to new heights.

Networking events provide a unique opportunity for freelancers to connect with potential clients face-to-face and build meaningful relationships. Attending industry-specific conferences, trade shows, seminars, or business networking events allows you to showcase your expertise and leave a lasting impression. Be prepared with business cards and a compelling elevator pitch that succinctly introduces yourself and your services. By engaging in conversations and exchanging contact information, you can expand your network and open doors to exciting collaborations and referrals.

Collaborating with local businesses is another effective offline marketing strategy. By partnering with complementary businesses in your area, you can cross-promote each other's services and tap into their existing client base. For example, a freelance graphic designer can collaborate with a local printing shop to offer joint packages or referrals. This not only expands your reach but also showcases your commitment to supporting local businesses and fosters a sense of community.

Public speaking engagements are a powerful way to establish yourself as an authority in your field and connect with potential clients. Offer to speak at industry events, workshops, or business organizations, sharing your expertise and providing valuable insights. Tailor your presentations to address the needs and challenges of your target audience, offering tangible takeaways that make an impact. By providing valuable insights and showcasing your knowledge, you position yourself as a trusted resource and attract potential clients who may be in the audience.

Print advertising may seem old-fashioned in the digital age, but it can still be an effective offline marketing strategy for freelancers. Consider placing advertisements in local newspapers, magazines, or relevant trade publications that are read by your target audience. Craft compelling ad copy that highlights your unique value proposition and includes your contact information or website. By strategically placing your ads, you can capture the attention of potential clients who may not have discovered you online.

Direct mail campaigns offer a personalized touch that can set you apart from the competition. Design and send targeted direct mail campaigns to potential clients in your area, highlighting the value you can provide. Personalize your messages and include a call-to-action, such as requesting a free consultation or visiting your website for more information. By showing that you've taken the time to reach out directly, you demonstrate your commitment to providing exceptional service.

Community involvement is a powerful way to raise awareness of your freelance services and build trust within your local community. Engage in community activities, volunteer for relevant causes, participate in local business organizations, or support community initiatives. By being visible and active in the community, you can build relationships, generate referrals, and establish yourself as a trusted professional. This sense of community involvement can make a lasting impression on potential clients and set you apart from the competition.

Client testimonials and case studies are valuable tools in your offline marketing arsenal. Collect testimonials from satisfied clients and develop case studies that highlight successful projects you've completed. Utilize these materials in offline marketing materials, such as brochures or presentations, to showcase the value you bring to clients. By providing social proof and tangible examples of your expertise, you instill confidence in potential clients and demonstrate your ability to deliver results.

Referral programs are an effective way to harness the power of word-of-mouth marketing. Implement a referral program where you reward existing clients or contacts who refer new business to you. This not only incentivizes people to recommend your services but also helps you tap into their networks and expand your reach. By actively encouraging referrals and expressing gratitude for them, you foster a sense of loyalty and strengthen your relationships with existing clients.

Remember, offline marketing strategies should be integrated with online efforts for maximum impact. Include your website or social media profiles on printed materials and encourage potential clients to connect with you online for more information. By adopting these offline marketing strategies, freelancers can increase their visibility, establish credibility, and connect with potential clients in meaningful ways. The key is to identify the most effective offline channels for reaching your target audience and consistently promote your services while delivering value and building relationships.

In the world of freelancing, it's easy to get lost in the digital noise. But by exploring offline marketing strategies, you can cut through the clutter and make a lasting impression on potential clients. Networking events, collaborations with local businesses, public speaking engagements, print advertising, direct mail campaigns, community involvement, client testimonials, case studies, and referral programs are all powerful tools at your disposal. By leveraging these opportunities, you can expand your network, establish yourself as an authority in your field, and attract high-quality clients. So step out from behind your computer screen and embrace the world of offline marketing. The rewards are waiting for you.

CHAPTER 16

Balancing Multiple Clients and Projects

As a freelancer, one of the biggest challenges you may face is managing multiple clients and projects simultaneously. It requires strong organizational skills, efficient time management, and effective communication. In this chapter, we will explore strategies and techniques to help you effectively handle the juggling act of balancing multiple clients and projects. By implementing these strategies, you can ensure the successful completion of each project while maintaining client satisfaction.

Prioritize and Set Clear Goals:

The first step in managing multiple clients and projects is to prioritize and set clear goals. Start by prioritizing your clients and projects based on deadlines, importance, or revenue potential. This will help you allocate your time and resources effectively. Set clear goals and objectives for each project to stay focused and ensure that you are working towards specific outcomes.

Utilize Project Management Tools:

To keep track of tasks, deadlines, and project progress, it is essential to utilize project management tools. Platforms like Trello, Asana, or Monday.com can help you stay organized, collaborate with clients or team members, and visualize project timelines. These tools allow you to break down projects into smaller tasks, assign deadlines, and monitor progress effectively.

Create a Schedule and Stick to It:

Establishing a schedule is crucial for managing multiple clients and projects. Allocate dedicated time for each client and project by setting specific working hours for different tasks. For example, you can designate certain hours for client communication, research, or project development. By sticking to the schedule, you ensure that you allocate sufficient time for all your commitments.

Communicate Expectations and Deadlines:

Clear communication is key when managing multiple clients and projects. Communicate expectations, deliverables, and deadlines with your clients upfront. Make sure they understand the timeline and any potential limitations. Regularly update clients on project progress and address any issues or delays proactively to manage their expectations effectively.

Delegate or Outsource When Necessary:

If you find yourself overwhelmed with multiple projects, consider delegating or outsourcing certain tasks to other freelancers or professionals. This can help alleviate your workload and ensure that each project receives proper attention. Identify tasks that are non-core or outside your expertise and find reliable individuals or service providers to handle them.

Practice Effective Time Management Techniques:

Implementing time management techniques is crucial for balancing multiple clients and projects. Techniques like the Pomodoro Technique or time blocking can increase focus and productivity. The Pomodoro Technique involves working in focused bursts of 25 minutes followed by short breaks. Time blocking involves assigning specific time blocks for different tasks or clients throughout the day. These techniques help you manage your time effectively and prevent burnout.

Maintain Open Communication Channels:

Establish clear channels of communication with your clients to facilitate effective and timely communication. Utilize email, phone calls, instant messaging, or project management platforms to ensure that clients can reach you easily when needed. Prompt communication helps build trust and ensures that you are responsive to clients' needs.

Manage Client Expectations:

Transparency is key when managing multiple clients and projects. Be honest about your availability, workload, and turnaround times. Set realistic expectations with clients regarding response times and project delivery. Managing expectations upfront helps prevent misunderstandings and ensures a smoother client experience.

Practice Self-Care:

To maintain focus, productivity, and overall well-being, it is crucial to prioritize self-care. Take breaks, exercise, get enough sleep, and engage in activities that help relax your mind. By taking care of yourself, you stay energized and better equipped to handle multiple clients and projects.

Balancing multiple clients and projects as a freelancer requires careful planning, effective time management, and strong communication skills. By prioritizing tasks, utilizing project management tools, setting clear goals, and practicing efficient time management techniques, you can effectively manage multiple clients and projects simultaneously. Additionally, maintaining open communication channels, managing client expectations, and prioritizing self-care are essential for maintaining client satisfaction and your own well-being. With these strategies in place, you can successfully navigate the challenges of freelancing and thrive in your career.

CHAPTER 17

Maintaining Work-Life Balance

Maintaining a healthy work-life balance is crucial for freelancers to avoid burnout, enhance productivity, and ensure overall well-being. In this chapter, we will explore strategies to help freelancers achieve a healthy work-life balance, including setting clear boundaries, prioritizing self-care, planning and scheduling, learning to say no, delegating non-core tasks, disconnecting from technology, practicing time management techniques, and regularly evaluating and adjusting. By implementing these strategies, freelancers can create boundaries, prioritize self-care, and enjoy a fulfilling personal and professional life.

Setting Clear Boundaries:

Establishing clear boundaries between work and personal life is essential for maintaining a healthy work-life balance. Freelancers should define specific working hours and communicate them to clients, team members, and family members. By sticking to these boundaries, freelancers can create a separation between work and personal time, allowing them to fully engage in both aspects of their lives.

Prioritizing Self-Care:

Making self-care a priority is crucial for freelancers to recharge and maintain a healthy mindset. Engaging in activities that promote physical and mental well-being, such as exercise, meditation, hobbies, spending time with loved ones, or pursuing personal interests, can help freelancers avoid burnout and enhance their overall well-being.

Planning and Scheduling:

Planning work and personal activities in advance is key to achieving a healthy work-life balance. By creating a schedule that allows for dedicated time for work, breaks, and personal activities, freelancers can ensure that they have a balanced allocation of time for both work and personal life.

Learning to Say No:

Learning to say no to projects, tasks, or commitments that do not align with desired work-life balance is essential. By being selective about the projects freelancers take on and focusing on those that align with their goals and values, they can maintain a healthier work-life balance and avoid overcommitting themselves.

Delegating Non-Core Tasks:

Delegating or outsourcing non-core tasks that consume too much time or cause unnecessary stress can free up time for personal activities. By focusing on their core strengths and priorities, freelancers can maintain a healthy work-life balance while ensuring that all necessary tasks are handled efficiently.

Disconnecting from Technology:

Setting aside designated periods to disconnect from technology helps create mental space and prevents work from encroaching on personal time. By turning off notifications or setting specific times for checking emails or messages, freelancers can create boundaries and ensure that personal time is fully dedicated to relaxation and rejuvenation.

Practicing Time Management Techniques:

Utilizing time management techniques such as the Pomodoro Technique or time blocking can enhance focus and productivity during work hours. Breaking tasks into manageable chunks and allocating specific time blocks for different activities allows freelancers to stay organized and make the most of their working hours.

Regularly Evaluating and Adjusting:

Regularly evaluating work-life balance and making adjustments as needed is crucial for maintaining a healthy balance that works for freelancers. By assessing workload, priorities, and overall well-being, freelancers can make necessary changes to ensure that they are achieving a healthy work-life balance.

Achieving a healthy work-life balance is an ongoing effort that requires conscious choices and regular self-reflection. By setting clear boundaries, prioritizing self-care, planning and scheduling, learning to say no, delegating non-core tasks, disconnecting from technology, practicing time management techniques, and regularly evaluating and adjusting, freelancers can create a balanced and fulfilling personal and professional life. By implementing these strategies, freelancers can maintain their well-being, enhance productivity, and enjoy the benefits of a healthy work-life balance.

CHAPTER 18

Navigating Freelancing During Economic Downturns

In the ever-changing landscape of freelancing, economic downturns can pose significant challenges for freelancers. However, with the right strategies and mindset, it is possible to navigate these uncertain times and maintain a stable income. In this chapter, we will explore the various strategies that freelancers can employ to thrive during economic downturns, as well as share real-life examples of freelancers who have successfully adapted their businesses. Additionally, we will discuss the importance of financial management practices and the mindset that freelancers should adopt to stay resilient in the face of economic challenges.

Diversify Your Client Base:

One of the key strategies for freelancers to navigate economic downturns is to diversify their client base. Relying on a few clients or industries can leave freelancers vulnerable during times of economic uncertainty. By seeking clients from different industries or sectors, freelancers can mitigate the risk of losing significant income if one industry is heavily affected by the downturn. This diversification allows freelancers to tap into various client needs and maintain a stable income.

For example, a graphic designer who also offers branding or marketing strategy services can attract clients looking to navigate challenging times. By being adaptable and versatile in their offerings, freelancers can attract new clients and maintain a stable income even during economic downturns.

Foster Client Relationships:

Nurturing relationships with existing clients is another crucial strategy for freelancers during economic downturns. While clients may reduce their budgets or projects during these times, maintaining strong relationships can lead to continued work or referrals. Frequent communication, providing value, and offering support are essential in strengthening these relationships. By prioritizing client relationships, freelancers can increase the likelihood of retaining clients and securing future projects.

Seek New Opportunities:

Actively seeking new opportunities is vital for freelancers during economic downturns. This can be done by attending virtual networking events, joining online communities, and leveraging social media platforms to connect with potential clients or collaborators. By being proactive in identifying emerging trends or niches, freelancers can position themselves for business opportunities that may arise during challenging times.

Offer Flexible Pricing or Payment Options:

During economic downturns, some clients may be more price-sensitive or have cash flow constraints. To accommodate their needs while ensuring a stable income, freelancers can consider offering flexible pricing models or payment plans. This flexibility can attract new clients and retain existing ones, providing freelancers with a steady stream of income even in uncertain times.

Build an Emergency Fund:

Establishing an emergency fund during prosperous times is crucial for freelancers to have a financial cushion during lean periods. By setting aside a portion of their income regularly, freelancers can create a buffer that can support them during economic uncertainties. This emergency fund provides peace of mind and stability, allowing freelancers to focus on their work without worrying about financial insecurities.

Invest in Professional Development:

Utilizing downtime during economic downturns to invest in professional development is a wise strategy for freelancers. By expanding their skills, updating their knowledge, or pursuing certifications, freelancers can make themselves more marketable and adaptable to changing client needs. This investment in professional development not only enhances their expertise but also positions them for continued success during economic downturns.

Collaborate with Other Freelancers:

Exploring collaboration opportunities with fellow freelancers who complement their skills or services is another way freelancers can thrive during economic downturns. By joining forces, freelancers can leverage each other's networks, share resources, and pursue larger projects together. Collaborations not only expand their client base but also provide a competitive advantage in the freelance market.

Stay Informed and Adaptable:

Staying updated on industry trends, economic forecasts, and shifts in client needs is crucial for freelancers during economic downturns. This enables them to anticipate changes and adapt their services accordingly. By being proactive and responsive to market demands, freelancers can position themselves for continued success even during challenging times.

Navigating freelancing during economic downturns requires adaptability, innovation, and proactive measures. By diversifying their client base, fostering client relationships, seeking new opportunities, offering flexible pricing, building an emergency fund, investing in professional development, collaborating with other freelancers, and staying informed and adaptable, freelancers can navigate economic downturns more effectively and maintain a stable income. With the right strategies and mindset, freelancers can not only survive but thrive during uncertain times, positioning themselves for long-term success in the freelance market.

CHAPTER 19

Embracing Change and Evolving as a Freelancer

Change is an inevitable part of life, and the freelancing industry is no exception. As the landscape evolves, freelancers must adapt to stay ahead of the curve and remain competitive. In this chapter, we will explore the strategies and steps that freelancers can take to embrace change and continually evolve in their careers.

To begin, freelancers must stay updated with industry trends. Actively researching and monitoring emerging technologies, best practices, and market trends allows freelancers to anticipate changes and adjust their skills, services, or marketing strategies accordingly. By staying informed, freelancers can position themselves as forward-thinking professionals who are prepared to meet the evolving needs of their clients.

Embracing new technologies and tools is another crucial aspect of adapting to change in the freelancing industry. Technology plays a significant role in enhancing productivity, efficiency, and service offerings. Freelancers should stay informed about new tools, software, and platforms that can give them a competitive edge. By adopting these technologies, freelancers can streamline their workflows, deliver higher-quality work, and attract clients who value innovation.

A culture of continuous learning is essential for freelancers to adapt to evolving client demands and industry trends. Cultivating a mindset of continuous learning can include taking online courses, attending webinars or conferences, reading industry publications, and participating in professional communities. By investing in their personal and professional growth, freelancers can stay ahead of the curve and offer clients the latest skills and knowledge.

Specializing in niche markets is becoming increasingly crucial in the competitive freelancing industry. By focusing on a specific niche or industry, freelancers can position themselves as experts in that field. This specialization attracts clients seeking specialized skills and knowledge, allowing freelancers to stand out from the crowd. By becoming a go-to expert in their niche, freelancers can command higher rates and build a reputation for excellence.

Building a personal brand is another essential aspect of adapting to change as a freelancer. Establishing a strong personal brand allows freelancers to differentiate themselves in a crowded marketplace. This involves crafting a compelling value proposition, showcasing expertise through a professional website and portfolio, and leveraging social media platforms to engage with the target audience. By building a strong personal brand, freelancers can attract clients who resonate with their unique offerings and values.

Cultivating a strong network is critical for freelancers to stay ahead of the curve. Building relationships with other freelancers, industry professionals, and potential clients provides valuable insights, collaboration opportunities, and referrals. Networking allows freelancers to stay informed about industry changes, gain support from peers, and access new opportunities. By actively nurturing their network, freelancers can stay connected and adapt to the evolving needs of their clients.

As the freelancing industry evolves, so do pricing structures and business models. Freelancers must stay abreast of these changes and evaluate whether alternative pricing models, such as value-based pricing or subscription-based services, align with their business goals. Adapting pricing and business models to meet changing client expectations ensures that freelancers remain competitive and financially sustainable in an evolving marketplace.

Clients increasingly seek freelancers who can provide end-to-end solutions rather than individual services. To adapt, freelancers can offer bundled or comprehensive solutions by collaborating with other freelancers or expanding their skill set. By providing holistic packages that address client needs, freelancers can position themselves as valuable partners who can handle all aspects of a project. This adaptability allows freelancers to meet the evolving demands of clients and stay ahead of the competition.

Seeking feedback from clients and peers is crucial for freelancers to understand their strengths and areas for improvement. Feedback enables freelancers to refine their skills, services, and processes to meet changing client expectations. By continuously seeking feedback, freelancers can adapt and improve, ensuring their work remains relevant and valuable in an ever-changing industry.

The COVID-19 pandemic has accelerated the shift towards remote work. Freelancers must adapt to remote work trends by embracing remote work tools and practices, improving virtual communication skills, and creating a conducive home workspace. By embracing remote work, freelancers can thrive in this new work environment and continue to deliver exceptional results for their clients.

Embracing change and evolving as a freelancer is essential for long-term success in the industry. By staying updated with industry trends, embracing new technologies, fostering a culture of continuous learning, specializing in niche markets, building a personal brand, cultivating a strong network, adapting pricing and business models, offering bundled solutions, seeking feedback, and adapting to remote work trends, freelancers can stay ahead of the curve and remain competitive in an evolving marketplace.

Freelancing is a dynamic and ever-changing field, and those who embrace change and continually evolve are the ones who will thrive. By adapting to industry changes, freelancers can position themselves as valuable assets to clients, enhance their competitiveness, and open doors for new opportunities. Embrace change, embrace growth, and embrace the future as a freelancer.

CHAPTER 20

Celebrating Success and Finding Fulfillment

As freelancers, it is important for us to recognize and celebrate our milestones and achievements. This chapter will explore the significance of celebrating success and finding fulfillment in our freelance careers. We will discuss the reasons why it is essential to acknowledge our accomplishments, reflect on our personal growth, and cultivate a positive mindset. Through personal experiences and examples, we will see how freelancers have found fulfillment in their work and how it has impacted their lives. Finally, we will provide strategies for maintaining a positive mindset and celebrating success throughout our careers.

Recognizing and celebrating milestones and achievements is vital for freelancers for several reasons. Firstly, it boosts motivation and confidence. By acknowledging our hard work and progress, we reinforce our belief in our abilities and fuel our drive to continue pushing forward. Secondly, celebrating milestones allows us to reflect on how far we have come. It provides an opportunity to assess our progress, highlighting the milestones we have achieved along the way. This reflection provides valuable insights into our growth, learning, and areas for further development.

Moreover, recognizing achievements helps us build a positive perception of our worth and value. It validates our skills, expertise, and contributions, reinforcing a strong sense of self-worth. This confidence can be an asset when negotiating rates, attracting clients, and pursuing new opportunities. Additionally, celebrating milestones cultivates a positive mindset and fosters a culture of success. It shifts our focus from potential setbacks or challenges to the achievements and progress we have made. This positive mindset can help us overcome obstacles and approach future projects or goals with optimism.

Furthermore, recognizing and celebrating milestones can have a positive impact on how clients perceive us. When we highlight our achievements, it demonstrates professionalism, expertise, and a track record of success. Clients are more likely to trust and value freelancers who have a proven history of delivering results. Additionally, celebrating milestones provides opportunities for us to showcase our achievements in our marketing efforts. We can update our portfolios, websites, or social media profiles to highlight completed projects, client testimonials, or significant milestones. This enhanced branding can attract new clients who are impressed by our track record.

Celebrating milestones can also lead to networking opportunities and potential collaborations. By sharing achievements within professional communities or attending industry events, we may catch the attention of like-minded professionals or potential collaborators looking for someone with our level of expertise. Moreover, celebrating milestones is crucial for maintaining work-life balance and overall well-being as a freelancer. By acknowledging our accomplishments, we can take time to rest, rejuvenate, and celebrate personal successes alongside professional ones. This helps prevent burnout and promotes a healthier work-life integration.

To reflect on our personal growth and find fulfillment in our freelance careers, we must follow these steps. Firstly, we need to set meaningful goals that align with our values, passions, and long-term aspirations. These goals should go beyond financial targets and encompass personal growth, skill development, and work-life balance. Secondly, we should regularly assess our progress towards our goals, reflecting on our achievements, challenges, and lessons learned. This self-reflection allows us to recognize how far we have come and identify areas for improvement or adjustment.

Additionally, celebrating milestones and achievements along the way is crucial. We should take time to acknowledge our accomplishments, both big and small. This recognition reinforces a sense of progress and boosts motivation. Embracing continuous learning is another important aspect of finding fulfillment in our freelance careers. By acquiring new skills, staying updated with industry trends, and seeking out learning opportunities, we can continuously invest in our professional development. This commitment to growth enhances personal fulfillment and keeps us engaged in our freelance career.

Seeking feedback from clients, peers, or mentors is also essential. It provides valuable insights into our strengths, blind spots, and areas for improvement. Engaging in mentorship relationships can help us receive guidance and advice from experienced professionals who can help us navigate our freelance journey. Moreover, finding meaning in our work is crucial for fulfillment. We should connect with the purpose behind our work and the impact it has on others. Reflecting on how our skills and services contribute to solving problems or fulfilling needs for our clients enhances fulfillment and satisfaction.

Cultivating work-life balance is another important aspect of finding fulfillment. We should prioritize work-life balance to avoid burnout and maintain overall well-being. Setting boundaries, establishing a routine, and making time for activities outside of work that bring us joy and fulfillment is essential. Engaging in collaboration and networking is also beneficial. By connecting with other freelancers, professionals, or industry communities, we can foster collaboration, share experiences, and expand our network. Connecting with like-minded individuals helps create a sense of belonging and support within the freelance community.

Finding joy and satisfaction in our work on a daily basis is crucial for maintaining motivation and overall well-being. There are several strategies we can implement to cultivate joy and satisfaction in our work. Firstly, we should choose projects wisely, selecting those that align with our interests and strengths. Working on projects that resonate with us and excite us will naturally bring more joy and satisfaction to our daily work. Secondly, practicing mindfulness in our work is important. By being fully present and engaged in the tasks at hand, we can focus on the process, enjoy the small victories, and appreciate the progress we make each day.

Setting realistic expectations is another strategy for finding joy and satisfaction in our work. Overcommitting or constantly feeling overwhelmed can lead to stress and dissatisfaction. Prioritizing our tasks, managing our time effectively, and maintaining a healthy work-life balance is crucial. Moreover, finding meaning in our work is essential. We should connect with the purpose behind our work and its impact on others. Reflecting on how our skills and services contribute to solving problems or fulfilling needs for our clients brings a sense of fulfillment and satisfaction.

Celebrating our accomplishments is another important strategy. We should acknowledge and celebrate our daily accomplishments, no matter how small. Taking a moment to reflect on what we have achieved each day and giving ourselves credit for our efforts is crucial. Seeking variety in our work is also beneficial. By taking on diverse projects or exploring different aspects of our industry, we can prevent monotony and keep ourselves engaged and excited about our work.

Building positive relationships with clients, peers, and collaborators is also important. Surrounding ourselves with supportive and inspiring individuals enhances job satisfaction and creates a sense of community. Embracing learning opportunities is another strategy. By embracing opportunities for learning and growth within our work, we challenge ourselves to acquire new skills, explore new technologies, or take on projects that push us beyond our comfort zone. The process of learning and improving brings joy and satisfaction.

Expressing creativity in our work is another important aspect of finding joy and satisfaction. By finding innovative solutions, exploring new ideas, or infusing our personal style into our projects, we allow ourselves to express creativity and bring a sense of joy and fulfillment. Taking breaks and practicing self-care is also crucial. Incorporating regular breaks into our workday to recharge and avoid burnout, prioritizing self-care activities that bring us joy, and taking care of ourselves enhance our overall well-being and help maintain a positive mindset.

Maintaining a positive mindset and celebrating success throughout our freelance careers is essential. By practicing gratitude, setting realistic goals, reflecting on achievements, embracing positive self-talk, surrounding ourselves with supportive peers, taking breaks, and practicing self-care, we can cultivate a positive mindset. Creating rituals for celebration, seeking feedback, and learning from setbacks are also important strategies. By implementing these strategies, we can maintain a positive mindset and celebrate success throughout our freelance careers.

Recognizing and celebrating milestones and achievements is vital for freelancers. It boosts motivation, builds confidence, reflects progress, enhances self-worth, shapes client perception, supports marketing efforts, fosters collaboration opportunities, contributes to work-life balance, and promotes a positive mindset. Reflecting on our personal growth, finding fulfillment in our freelance careers, and maintaining a positive mindset are crucial for our overall well-being and success. By following the strategies outlined in this chapter, we can find joy and satisfaction in our work on a daily basis and celebrate our successes along the way.

CHAPTER 21

Looking Ahead: The Future of Freelancing

As the freelance industry continues to grow and evolve, it is essential for freelancers to stay ahead of the curve and prepare for the future. The landscape of freelancing is dynamic and subject to ongoing changes influenced by factors such as market dynamics, technological advancements, economic conditions, and societal shifts. In this chapter, we will explore the trends and predictions for the future of freelancing and discuss the strategies and skills freelancers can develop to thrive in this evolving landscape.

The future of freelancing holds immense potential for growth and opportunity. With the rise of remote work, advancements in technology, and changing attitudes towards traditional employment, the freelance industry is expected to continue its upward trajectory. Freelancers can embrace this gig economy and remote work opportunities by leveraging online platforms and marketplaces that connect them with clients seeking their specific skills. By creating a compelling profile, showcasing their expertise, and actively bidding or pitching for relevant projects, freelancers can tap into a global marketplace of clients and projects.

Specialization and niche expertise will become increasingly important in the competitive freelance market. Clients will seek freelancers who have deep knowledge and experience in specific industries or skills, allowing them to provide highly tailored solutions. To stay ahead, freelancers should continuously assess industry trends, identify emerging opportunities, and adapt their skills or services accordingly.

Online gig platforms and marketplaces will continue to play a significant role in connecting freelancers with clients. These platforms will evolve to offer more advanced features, such as AI-powered matching algorithms, enhanced project management tools, and integrated payment systems. Freelancers should leverage these platforms to expand their reach, connect with clients, and streamline their workflow.

The COVID-19 pandemic has accelerated the adoption of remote work and virtual collaboration. This trend is likely to continue, with freelancers leveraging remote collaboration tools and video conferencing platforms to work with clients from anywhere in the world. The ability to work remotely and collaborate virtually will lead to increased globalization of freelance talent. Companies will have access to a global pool of freelancers, allowing them to leverage diverse perspectives, cultural insights, and specialized skills from various regions.

The line between traditional employment and freelancing will become increasingly blurred as more companies adopt hybrid models that combine full-time employees with freelance talent. This shift allows businesses to access specialized skills on-demand while maintaining core teams. Freelancers should be prepared to navigate this evolving landscape and position themselves as valuable contributors to these hybrid work environments.

Automation and artificial intelligence will impact the freelance industry, particularly in areas such as content generation, data analysis, customer support, and repetitive tasks. Freelancers will need to adapt by upskilling in areas that complement automation or by focusing on uniquely human skills that cannot be easily automated. Emphasis on personal branding will become even more critical for freelancers to stand out from the competition. Building a strong personal brand through marketing efforts, online presence, and thought leadership will showcase their expertise and attract clients.

As the freelance workforce grows, there is a growing focus on gig worker rights, protections, and benefits. Freelancers may see increased advocacy for fair pay, access to healthcare, retirement savings options, and other benefits traditionally associated with full-time employment. It is important for freelancers to stay informed about these developments and advocate for their rights in the industry.

The rapid pace of technological advancements will require freelancers to engage in continuous learning and skill development to stay relevant. Lifelong learning will become crucial for freelancers to adapt to changing market demands and acquire new skills as needed. Freelancers should invest in professional development, stay updated with industry trends, and be willing to learn new technologies or tools.

The future of freelancing holds immense potential for growth and opportunity. Freelancers can embrace this future by staying adaptable, continuously learning and evolving, building strong client relationships, and providing exceptional service. By staying informed about industry trends, investing in skill development, and proactively adapting to changes, freelancers can position themselves for success in the evolving freelance landscape. The key to thriving in this dynamic industry is to embrace the gig economy and remote work opportunities with a positive mindset, continuously learn and evolve, communicate effectively, build strong relationships, and provide exceptional service. So, gear up and embrace the future of freelancing with confidence and enthusiasm!

ABOUT THE AUTHOR

Zach C. Andy

Zach C. Andy is not just an author, but a beacon of guidance for those looking to enrich their personal and professional lives. A staunch advocate for personal development, Zach has dedicated his career to aiding individuals in their quest for resilience, balance, and success. His unique approach to self-help is rooted in practicality, offering readers strategies and techniques that are both effective and actionable.

With a series of successful books under his belt, Zach has proven his ability to understand and articulate the challenges that people face in their daily lives. His latest work, "From Side Hustle to Full-Time Gig: Freelancing 101," is a testament to his expertise in navigating the intricacies of modern work-life dynamics. This book is poised to be an indispensable resource for freelancers looking to make the leap into full-time entrepreneurship.

Zach's passion is evident in every page he writes, inspiring his readers to take control and make the changes necessary to lead a fulfilling life. His writings are more than just words; they are a call to action—a catalyst for transformation.

For those who have journeyed with Zach through his previous works, including "Unveiling Your True Worth: A Journey of Self-Discovery," "How to Overcome Procrastination & Boost Productivity," and "The Ultimate Guide to Stress Management Techniques," the path towards self-improvement has been both enlightening and empowering.

As you dive into the pages of Zach C. Andy's books, you join a community of learners and doers who are all seeking to unlock their potential and thrive in the face of life's challenges. Whether you are a seasoned reader of his works or are discovering his insights for the first time, you can expect a transformative experience that will leave you equipped to face whatever comes your way with confidence and poise.

BOOKS BY THIS AUTHOR

The Ultimate Guide To Stress Management Techniques

Discover the Ultimate Guide to Stress Management Techniques and unlock the power to navigate life's challenges with grace and resilience.

In today's fast-paced world, stress has become an all too common companion. Whether it's the demands of work, personal responsibilities, or the constant pressure to keep up with the ever-changing world around us, stress can take a toll on our physical and mental well-being.

"The Ultimate Guide to Stress Management Techniques" is a comprehensive resource that provides practical tools, strategies, and insights to help you effectively manage stress and find balance in your life. Authored by self-help author and personal development advocate Zach C. Andy, this guide combines research, personal experiences, and the wisdom of countless individuals who have triumphed over stress.

Through the chapters of this guide, you will explore various aspects of stress management, including identifying the causes and effects of stress, developing healthy coping mechanisms, building resilience, and fostering a positive mindset. From time management techniques to enhancing emotional well-being and creating a relaxation-friendly environment, you will discover a wide range of strategies that can be tailored to fit your unique circumstances and needs.

"The Ultimate Guide to Stress Management Techniques" is more than just a book; it is a roadmap for long-term growth and well-being. Each chapter offers practical guidance, reflective exercises, and actionable steps to help you navigate your personal journey towards stress management. With a commitment to self-awareness, self-care, and continuous learning, you can transform stress from a burden into an opportunity for growth.

Whether you are seeking ways to reduce stress, enhance resilience, or find inner peace, this guide will empower you to overcome obstacles, maximize your potential, and lead a life filled with balance and well-being. Join countless others who have discovered the transformative power of stress management techniques and unlock the path to a healthier, more fulfilling life.

Take control of your well-being today. Dive into "The Ultimate Guide to Stress Management Techniques" and embark on a journey towards mastering stress management, finding resilience, and embracing a life of harmony and tranquility.

How To Overcome Procrastination And Boost Productivity: Make Your Dreams A Reality From This Point Forward

"How to Overcome Procrastination and Boost Productivity" by Zach C. Andy is a transformative guide that offers practical strategies and insights to help you break free from the clutches of procrastination and unlock your true productivity potential. Through chapters that delve into the psychology behind procrastination, the concept of productivity, mindset shifts, creating effective action plans, building productive habits, overcoming roadblocks, and sustaining momentum, this book provides a comprehensive roadmap for achieving personal and professional success. Whether you struggle with perfectionism, fear of failure, lack of motivation, or difficulty managing distractions, this book equips you with the tools and mindset necessary to overcome these obstacles and take control of your time. With the guidance of Zach C. Andy, you'll discover how to cultivate a growth mindset, set clear goals, optimize your time management skills, and develop productive habits that will propel you towards your dreams. Embrace this journey towards increased productivity and fulfillment, and unlock your true potential today.

Unveiling Your True Worth: A Journey To Self-Discovery

Introducing "Unveiling Your True Worth: A Journey to Self-Discovery"! This profound book delves into the concept of self-worth and its impact on every aspect of our lives. It is designed to guide readers on a transformative journey, helping them understand, acknowledge, and elevate their self-worth.

Spanning ten comprehensive chapters, this book covers various facets of personal growth. It begins by unraveling the significance of self-worth, debunking common misconceptions, and providing practical steps for improvement. Each subsequent chapter builds upon this foundation, exploring topics like the power of positive thinking, effective communication skills, resilience in the face of challenges, and the practice of mindfulness.

What sets this book apart is its unique ability to seamlessly blend theory with real-life applications. Readers are not only introduced to essential personal growth concepts but are also treated to relatable examples, personal stories, and practical exercises that facilitate the integration of these ideas into everyday life.

"Unveiling Your True Worth" delves deep into the role of self-worth in personal relationships and career fulfillment. By emphasizing the intrinsic value of individuals, it encourages readers to seek out relationships and careers that reflect this recognition of self-value.

Written in an engaging and accessible style, this book serves as a roadmap for those yearning for a more fulfilling and authentic life. It is a valuable resource for individuals ready to break free from societal definitions of worth and embrace their unique, inherent value. With its profound insights, practical exercises, and actionable tips, "Unveiling Your True Worth" is an indispensable companion for anyone embarking on the journey of self-discovery and personal transformation.